Self Mastery Throug

by

CONTENTS

SELF MASTERY THROUGH CONSCIOUS AUTOSUGGESTION

Suggestion, or rather Autosuggestion, is quite a new subject, and yet at the same time it is as old as the world.

It is new in the sense that until now it has been wrongly studied and in consequence wrongly understood; it is old because it dates from the appearance of man on the earth. In fact autosuggestion is an instrument that we possess at birth, and in this instrument, or rather in this force, resides a marvelous and incalculable power, which according to circumstances produces the best or the worst results. Knowledge of this force is useful to each one of us, but it is peculiarly indispensable to doctors, magistrates, lawyers, and to those engaged in the work of education.

By knowing how to practise it consciously it is possible in the first place to avoid provoking in others bad autosuggestions which may have disastrous consequences, and secondly, consciously to provoke good ones instead, thus bringing physical health to the sick, and moral health to the neurotic and the erring, the unconscious victims of anterior autosuggestions, and to guide into the right path those who had a tendency to take the wrong one.

THE CONSCIOUS SELF AND THE UNCONSCIOUS SELF

In order to understand properly the phenomena of suggestion, or to speak more correctly of autosuggestion, it is necessary to know that two absolutely distinct selves exist within us. Both are intelligent, but while one is conscious the other is unconscious. For this reason the existence of the latter generally escapes notice. It is however easy to prove its existence if one merely takes the trouble to examine certain phenomena and to reflect a few moments upon them. Let us take for instance the following examples:

Every one has heard of somnambulism; every one knows that a somnambulist gets up at night without waking, leaves his room after either dressing himself or not, goes downstairs, walks along corridors, and after having executed certain acts or accomplished certain work, returns to his room, goes to bed again, and shows next day the greatest astonishment at finding work finished which he had left unfinished the day before.

It is however he himself who has done it without being aware of it. What force has his body obeyed if it is not an unconscious force, in fact his unconscious self?

Let us now examine the alas, too frequent case of a drunkard attacked by delirium tremens. As though seized with madness he picks up the nearest weapon, knife, hammer, or hatchet, as the case may be, and strikes furiously those who are unlucky enough to be in his vicinity. Once the attack is over, he recovers his senses and contemplates with horror the scene of carnage around him, without realizing that he himself is the author of it. Here again is it not the unconscious self which has caused the unhappy man to act in this way? [*]

[*] And what aversions, what ills we create for ourselves, everyone of us and in every domain by not "immediately" bringing into play "good conscious autosuggestions" against our "bad unconscious autosuggestions," thus bringing about the disappearance of all unjust suffering.

If we compare the conscious with the unconscious self we see that the conscious self is often possessed of a very unreliable memory while the unconscious self on the contrary is provided with a marvelous and impeccable memory which registers without our knowledge the smallest events, the least important acts of our existence. Further, it is credulous and accepts with unreasoning docility what it is told. Thus, as it is the unconscious that is responsible for the functioning of all our organs but the intermediary of the brain, a result is produced which may seem rather paradoxical to you: that is, if it believes that a certain organ functions well or ill or that we feel such and such an impression, the organ in question does indeed function well or ill, or we do feel that impression.

Not only does the unconscious self preside over the functions of our organism, but also over all our actions whatever they are. It is this that we call imagination, and it is this which, contrary to accepted opinion, always makes us act even, and above all, against our will when there is antagonism between these two forces.

WILL AND IMAGINATION

If we open a dictionary and look up the word "will", we find this definition: "The faculty of freely determining certain acts". We accept this definition as true and unattackable, although nothing could be more false. This will that we claim so proudly, always yields to the imagination. It is an absolute rule that admits of no exception.

"Blasphemy! Paradox!" you will exclaim. "Not at all! On the contrary, it is the purest truth," I shall reply.

In order to convince yourself of it, open your eyes, look round you and try to understand what you see. You will then come to the conclusion that what I tell you is not an idle theory, offspring of a sick brain but the simple expression of a fact.

Suppose that we place on the ground a plank 30 feet long by 1 foot wide. It is evident that everybody will be capable of going from one end to the other of this plank without stepping over the edge. But now change the conditions of the experiment, and imagine this plank placed at the height of the towers of a cathedral. Who then will be capable of advancing even a few feet along this narrow path? Could you hear me speak? Probably not. Before you had taken two steps you would begin to tremble, and in spite of every effort of your will you would be certain to fall to the ground.

Why is it then that you would not fall if the plank is on the ground, and why should you fall if it is raised to a height above the ground? Simply because in the first case you imagine that it is easy to go to the end of this plank, while in the second case you imagine that you cannot do so.

Notice that your will is powerless to make you advance; if you imagine that you cannot, it is absolutely impossible for you to do so. If tilers and carpenters are able to accomplish this feat, it is because they think they can do it.

Vertigo is entirely caused by the picture we make in our minds that we are going to fall. This picture transforms itself immediately into fact in spite of all the efforts of our will, and the more violent these efforts are, the quicker is the opposite to the desired result brought about.

Let us now consider the case of a person suffering from insomnia. If he does not make any effort to sleep, he will lie quietly in bed. If on the contrary he tries to force himself to sleep by his will, the more efforts he makes, the more restless he becomes.

Have you not noticed that the more you try to remember the name of a person which you have forgotten, the more it eludes you, until, substituting in your mind the idea "I shall remember in a minute" to the idea "I have forgotten", the name comes back to you of its own accord without the least effort?

Let those of you who are cyclists remember the days when you were learning to ride. You went along clutching the handle bars and frightened of falling. Suddenly catching sight of the smallest obstacle in the road you tried to avoid it, and the more efforts you made to do so, the more surely you rushed upon it.

Who has not suffered from an attack of uncontrollable laughter, which bursts out more violently the more one tries to control it?

What was the state of mind of each person in these different circumstances? "I do not want to fall but I cannot help doing so"; "I want to sleep but I cannot "; "I want to remember the name of Mrs. So and So, but I cannot "; "I want to avoid the obstacle, but I cannot "; "I want to stop laughing, but I cannot."

As you see, in each of these conflicts it is always the imagination which gains the victory over the will, without any exception.

To the same order of ideas belongs the case of the leader who rushes forward at the head of his troops and always carries them along with him, while the cry "Each man for himself!" is almost certain to cause a defeat. Why is this? It is because in the first case the men imagine that they must go forward, and in the second they imagine that they are conquered and must fly for their lives.

Panurge was quite aware of the contagion of example, that is to say the action of the imagination, when, to avenge himself upon a merchant on board the same boat, he bought his biggest sheep and threw it into the sea, certain beforehand that the entire flock would follow, which indeed happened.

We human beings have a certain resemblance to sheep, and involuntarily, we are irresistibly impelled to follow other people's examples, imagining that we cannot do otherwise.

I could quote a thousand other examples but I should fear to bore you by such an enumeration. I cannot however pass by in silence this fact which shows the enormous power of the imagination, or in other words of the unconscious in its struggle against the will.

There are certain drunkards who wish to give up drinking, but who cannot do so. Ask them, and they will reply in all sincerity that they desire to be sober, that drink disgusts them, but that they are irresistibly impelled to drink against their will, in spite of the harm they know it will do them.

In the same way certain criminals commit crimes in spite of themselves, and when they are asked why they acted so, they answer "I could not help it, something impelled me, it was stronger than I."

And the drunkard and the criminal speak the truth; they are forced to do what they do, for the simple reason they imagine they cannot prevent themselves from doing so. Thus we who are so proud of our will, who believe that we are free to act as we like, are in reality nothing but wretched puppets of which our imagination holds all the strings. We only cease to be puppets when we have learned to guide our imagination.

SUGGESTION AND AUTOSUGGESTION

According to the preceding remarks we can compare the imagination to a torrent which fatally sweeps away the poor wretch who has fallen into it, in spite of his efforts to gain the bank. This torrent seems indomitable; but if you know how, you can turn it from its course and conduct it to the factory, and there you can transform its force into movement, heat, and electricity.

If this simile is not enough, we may compare the imagination--"the madman at home" as it has been called--to an unbroken horse which has neither bridle nor reins. What can the rider do except let himself go wherever the horse wishes to take him? And often if the latter runs away, his mad career only comes to end in the ditch. If however the rider succeeds in putting a bridle on the horse, the parts are reversed. It is no longer the horse who goes where he likes, it is the rider who obliges the horse to take him wherever he wishes to go.

Now that we have learned to realize the enormous power of the unconscious or imaginative being, I am going to show how this self, hitherto considered indomitable, can be as easily controlled as a torrent or an unbroken horse. But before going any further it is necessary to define carefully two words that are often used without being properly understood. These are the words suggestion and autosuggestion.

What then is suggestion? It may be defined as "the act of imposing an idea on the brain of another". Does this action really exist? Properly speaking, no. Suggestion does not indeed exist by itself. It does not and cannot exist except on the sine qua non condition of transforming itself into autosuggestion in the subject. This latter word may be defined as "the implanting of an idea in oneself by oneself."

You may make a suggestion to someone; if the unconscious of the latter does not accept the suggestion, if it has not, as it were, digested it, in order to transform it into autosuggestion, it produces no result. I have myself occasionally made a more or less commonplace suggestion to ordinarily very obedient subjects quite unsuccessfully. The reason is that the unconscious of the subject refused to accept it and did not transform it into autosuggestion.

THE USE OF AUTOSUGGESTION

Let us now return to the point where I said that we can control and lead our imagination, just as a torrent or an unbroken horse can be controlled. To do so, it is enough in the first place to know that this is possible (of which fact almost everyone is ignorant) and secondly, to know by what means it can be done. Well, the means is very simple; it is that which we have used every day since we came into the world, without wishing or knowing it and absolutely unconsciously, but which unfortunately for us, we often use wrongly and to our own detriment. This means is autosuggestion.

Whereas we constantly give ourselves unconscious autosuggestions, all we have to do is to give ourselves conscious ones, and the process consists in this: first, to weigh carefully in one's mind the things which are to be the object of the autosuggestion, and according as they require the answer "yes" or "no" to repeat several times without thinking of anything else: "This thing is coming", or "this thing is going away"; "this thing will, or will not happen, etc., etc. . . ." [*] If the unconscious accepts this suggestion and transforms it into an autosuggestion, the thing or things are realized in every particular.

[*] Of course the thing must be in our power.

Thus understood, autosuggestion is nothing but hypnotism as I see it, and I would define it in these simple words: The influence of the imagination upon the moral and physical being of mankind. Now this influence is undeniable, and without returning to previous examples, I will quote a few others.

If you persuade yourself that you can do a certain thing, provided this thing be possible, you will do it however difficult it may be. If on the contrary you imagine that you cannot do the simplest thing in the world, it is impossible for you to do it, and molehills become for you unscalable mountains.

Such is the case of neurasthenics, who, believing themselves incapable of the least effort, often find it impossible even to walk a few steps without being exhausted. And these same neurasthenics sink more deeply into their depression, the more efforts they make to throw it off, like the poor wretch in the quicksands who sinks in all the deeper the more he tries to struggle out.

In the same way it is sufficient to think a pain is going, to feel it indeed disappear little by little, and inversely, it is enough to think that one suffers in order to feel the pain begin to come immediately.

I know certain people who predict in advance that they will have a sick headache on a certain day, in certain circumstances, and on that day, in the given circumstances, sure enough, they feel it. They brought their illness on themselves, just as others cure theirs by conscious autosuggestion.

I know that one generally passes for mad in the eyes of the world if one dares to put forward ideas which it is not accustomed to hear. Well, at the risk of being thought so, I say that if certain people are ill mentally and physically, it is that they imagine themselves to be ill mentally or physically. If certain others are paralytic without having any lesion to account for it, it is that they imagine themselves to be paralyzed, and it is among such persons that the most extraordinary cures are produced. If others again are happy or unhappy, it is that they imagine themselves to be so, for it is possible for two people in exactly the same circumstances to be, the one perfectly happy, the other absolutely wretched.

Neurasthenia, stammering, aversions, kleptomania, certain cases of paralysis, are nothing but the result of unconscious autosuggestion, that is to say the result of the action of the unconscious upon the physical and moral being.

But if our unconscious is the source of many of our ills, it can also bring about the cure of our physical and mental ailments. It can not only repair the ill it has done, but cure real illnesses, so strong is its action upon our organism.

Shut yourself up alone in a room, seat yourself in an armchair, close your eyes to avoid any distraction, and concentrate your mind for a few moments on thinking: "Such and such a thing is going to disappear", or "Such and such a thing is coming to pass."

If you have really made the autosuggestion, that is to say, if your unconscious has assimilated the idea that you have presented to it, you are astonished to see the thing you have thought come to pass. (Note that it is the property of ideas autosuggested to exist within us unrecognized, and we can only know of their existence by the effect they produce.) But above all, and this is an essential point, the will must not be brought into play in practising autosuggestion; for, if it is not in agreement with the imagination, if one thinks: "I will make such and such a thing happen", and the imagination says: "You are willing it, but it is not going to be", not only does one not obtain what one wants, but even exactly the reverse is brought about.

This remark is of capital importance, and explains why results are so unsatisfactory when, in treating moral ailments, one strives to re-educate the will. It is the training of the imagination which is necessary, and it is thanks to this shade of difference that my method has often succeeded where others-- and those not the least considered--have failed. From the numerous experiments that I have made daily for twenty years, and which I have examined with minute care, I have been able to deduct the following conclusions which I have summed up as laws:

1. When the will and the imagination are antagonistic, it is always the imagination which wins, without any exception.

2. In the conflict between the will and the imagination, the force of the imagination is in direct ratio to the square of the will.

3. When the will and the imagination are in agreement, one does not add to the other, but one is multiplied by the other.

4. The imagination can be directed.

(The expressions "In direct ratio to the square of the will" and "Is multiplied by" are not rigorously exact. They are simply illustrations destined to make my meaning clearer.)

After what has just been said it would seem that nobody ought to be ill. That is quite true. Every illness, whatever it may be, can yield to autosuggestion, daring and unlikely as my statement may seem; I do not say does always yield, but can yield, which is a different thing.

But in order to lead people to practise conscious autosuggestion they must be taught how, just as they are taught to read or write or play the piano.

Autosuggestion is, as I said above, an instrument that we possess at birth, and with which we play unconsciously all our life, as a baby plays with its rattle. It is however a dangerous instrument; it can wound or even kill you if you handle it imprudently and unconsciously. It can on the contrary save your life when you know how to employ it consciously. One can say of it as Aesop said of the tongue: "It is at the same time the best and the worst thing in the world".

I am now going to show you how everyone can profit by the beneficent action of autosuggestion consciously applied. In saying "every one", I exaggerate a little, for there are two classes of persons in whom it is difficult to arouse conscious autosuggestion:

1. The mentally undeveloped who are not capable of understanding what you say to them.

2. Those who are unwilling to understand.

HOW TO TEACH PATIENTS TO MAKE AUTOSUGGESTIONS

The principle of the method may be summed up in these few words: It is impossible to think of two things at once, that is to say that two ideas may be in juxtaposition, but they cannot be superimposed in our mind.

Every thought entirely filling our mind becomes true for us and tends to transform itself into action.

Thus if you can make a sick person think that her trouble is getting better, it will disappear; if you succeed in making a kleptomaniac think that he will not steal any more, he will cease to steal, etc., etc.

This training which perhaps seems to you an impossibility, is, however, the simplest thing in the world. It is enough, by a series of appropriate and graduated experiments, to teach the subject, as it were the A. B. C. of conscious thought, and here is the series: by following it to the letter one can be absolutely sure of obtaining a good result, except with the two categories of persons mentioned above.

First experiment.[*] Preparatory.--Ask the subject to stand upright, with the body as stiff as an iron bar, the feet close together from toe to heel, while keeping the ankles flexible as if they were hinges. Tell him to make himself like a plank with hinges at its base, which is balanced on the ground. Make him notice that if one pushes the plank slightly either way it falls as a mass without any resistance, in the direction in which it is pushed. Tell him that you are going to pull him back by the shoulders and that he must let himself fall in your arms without the slightest resistance, turning on his ankles as on hinges, that is to say keeping the feet fixed to the ground. Then pull him back by the shoulders and if the experiment does not succeed, repeat it until it does, or nearly so.

[*] These experiments are those of Sage of Rochester.

Second experiment.--Begin by explaining to the subject that in order to demonstrate the action of the imagination upon us, you are going to ask him in a moment to think: "I am falling backwards, I am falling backwards. . . ." Tell him that he must have no thought but this in his mind, that he must not reflect or wonder if he is going to fall or not, or think that if he falls he may hurt himself, etc., or fall back purposely to please you, but that if he really feels something impelling him to fall backwards, he must not resist but obey the impulse.

Then ask your subject to raise the head high and to shut his eyes, and place your right fist on the back of his neck, and your left hand on his forehead, and say to him: "Now think: I am falling backwards, I am falling backwards, etc., etc. . ." and, indeed, "You are falling backwards, You . . . are . . . fall . . . ing . . . back . . . wards, etc." At the same time slide the left hand lightly backwards to the left temple, above the ear, and remove very slowly but with a continuous movement the right fist.

The subject is immediately felt to make a slight movement backwards, and either to stop himself from falling or else to fall completely. In the first case, tell him that he has resisted, and that he did not think just that he was falling, but that he might hurt himself if he did fall. That is true, for if he had not thought the latter, he would have fallen like a block. Repeat the experiment using a tone of command as if you would force the subject to obey you. Go on with it until it is completely successful or very nearly so. The operator should stand a little behind the subject, the left leg forward and the right leg well behind him, so as not to be knocked over by the subject when he falls. Neglect of this precaution might result in a double fall if the person is heavy.

Third experiment.--Place the subject facing you, the body still stiff, the ankles flexible, and the feet joined and parallel. Put your two hands on his temples without any pressure, look fixedly, without moving the eyelids, at the root of his nose, and tell him to think: "I am falling forward, I am falling forward . . ." and repeat to him, stressing the syllables, "You are fall . . . ing . . . for . . . ward, You are fall . . . ing . . . for . . . ward . . ." without ceasing to look fixedly at him.

Fourth experiment.--Ask the subject to clasp his hands as tight as possible, that is to say, until the fingers tremble slightly, look at him in the same way as in the preceding experiment and keep your hands on his as though to squeeze them together still more tightly. Tell him to think that he cannot unclasp his fingers, that you are going to count three, and that when you say "three" he is to try to separate his hands while thinking all the time: "I cannot do it, I cannot do it . . ." and he will find it impossible. Then count very slowly, "one, two, three", and add immediately, detaching the syllables: "You . . . can . . . not . . . do . . . it. . . . You . . . can . . . not . . . do . . . it. . . ." If the subject is thinking properly, "I cannot do it", not only is he unable to separate his fingers, but the latter clasp themselves all the more tightly together the more efforts he makes to separate them. He obtains in fact exactly the contrary to what he wants. In a few moments say to him: "Now think: 'I can do it,'" and his fingers will separate themselves.

Be careful always to keep your eyes fixed on the root of the subject's nose, and do not allow him to turn his eyes away from yours for a single moment. If he is able to unclasp his hands, do not think it is your own fault, it is the subject's, he has not properly thought: "I cannot". Assure him firmly of this, and begin the experiment again.

Always use a tone of command which suffers no disobedience. I do not mean that it is necessary to raise your voice; on the contrary it is preferable to employ the ordinary pitch, but stress every word in a dry and imperative tone.

When these experiments have been successful, all the others succeed equally well and can be easily obtained by carrying out to the letter the instructions given above.

Some subjects are very sensitive, and it is easy to recognize them by the fact that the contraction of their fingers and limbs is easily produced. After two or three successful experiments, it is no longer necessary to say to them: "Think this", or "think that"; You need only, for example, say to them simply--but in the imperative tone employed by all good suggestionists--"Close your hands; now you cannot open them". "Shut your eyes; now you cannot open them," and the subject finds it absolutely impossible to open the hands or the eyes in spite of all his efforts. Tell him in a few moments: "You can do it now," and the de-contraction takes place instantaneously.

These experiments can be varied to infinity. Here are a few more: Make the subject join his hands, and suggest that they are welded together; make him put his hand on the table, and suggest that it is stuck to it; tell him that he is fixed to his chair and cannot rise; make him rise, and tell him he cannot walk; put a penholder on the table and tell him that it weighs a hundredweight, and that he cannot lift it, etc., etc.

In all these experiments, I cannot repeat too often, it is not suggestion properly so-called which produces the phenomena, but the autosuggestion which is consecutive to the suggestion of the operator.

METHOD OF PROCEDURE IN CURATIVE SUGGESTION

When the subject has passed through the preceding experiments and has understood them, he is ripe for curative suggestion. He is like a cultivated field in which the seed can germinate and develop, whereas before it was but rough earth in which it would have perished.

Whatever ailment the subject suffers from, whether it is physical or mental, it is important to proceed always in the same way, and to use the same words with a few variations according to the case.

Say to the subject: Sit down and close your eyes. I am not going to try and put you to sleep as it is quite unnecessary. I ask you to close your eyes simply in order that your attention may not be distracted by the objects around you. Now tell yourself that every word I say is going to fix itself in your mind, and be printed, engraved, and encrusted in it, that, there, it is going to stay fixed, imprinted, and encrusted, and that without your will or knowledge, in fact perfectly unconsciously on your part, you yourself and your whole organism are going to obey. In the first place I say that every day, three times a day, in the morning, at midday, and in the evening, at the usual meal times, you will feel hungry, that is to say, you will experience the agreeable sensation which makes you think and say: "Oh! how nice it will be to have something to eat!" You will then eat and enjoy your food, without of course overeating. You will also be careful to masticate it properly so as to transform it into a sort of soft paste before swallowing it. In these conditions you will digest it properly, and so feel no discomfort, inconvenience, or pain of any kind either in the stomach or intestines. You will assimilate what you eat and your organism will make use of it to make blood, muscle, strength and energy, in a word: Life.

Since you will have digested your food properly, the function of excretion will be normal, and every morning, on rising, you will feel the need of evacuating the bowels, and without ever being obliged to take medicine or to use any artifice, you will obtain a normal and satisfactory result.

Further, every night from the time you wish to go to sleep till the time you wish to wake next morning, you will sleep deeply, calmly, and quietly, without nightmares, and on waking you will feel perfectly well, cheerful, and active.

Likewise, if you occasionally suffer from depression, if you are gloomy and prone to worry and look on the dark side of things, from now onwards you will cease to do so, and, instead of worrying and being depressed and looking on the dark side of things, you are going to feel perfectly cheerful, possibly without any special reason for it, just as you used to feel depressed for no particular reason. I say further still, that even if you have real reason to be worried and depressed you are not going to be so.

If you are also subject to occasional fits of impatience or ill-temper you will cease to have them: on the contrary you will be always patient and master of yourself, and the things which worried, annoyed, or irritated you, will henceforth leave you absolutely indifferent and perfectly calm.

If you are sometimes attacked, pursued, haunted, by bad and unwholesome ideas, by apprehensions, fears, aversions, temptations, or grudges against other people, all that will be gradually lost sight of by your imagination, and will melt away and lose itself as though in a distant cloud where it will finally disappear completely. As a dream vanishes when we wake, so will all these vain images disappear.

To this I add that all your organs are performing their functions properly. The heart beats in a normal way and the circulation of the blood takes place as it should; the lungs are carrying out their functions, as also the stomach, the intestines, the liver, the biliary duct, the kidneys and the bladder. If at the present moment any of them is acting abnormally, that abnormality is becoming less every day, so that quite soon it will have vanished completely, and the organ will have recovered its normal function. Further, if there should be any lesions in any of these organs, they will get better from day to day and will soon be entirely healed. (With regard to this, I may say that it is not necessary to know which organ is affected for it to be cured. Under the influence of the autosuggestion "Every day, in every respect, I am getting better and better", the unconscious acts upon the organ which it can pick out itself.)

I must also add--and it is extremely important--that if up to the present you have lacked confidence in yourself, I tell you that this self-distrust will disappear little by little and give place to self-confidence, based on the knowledge of this force of incalculable power which is in each one of us. It is absolutely necessary for every human being to have this confidence. Without it one can accomplish nothing, with it one can accomplish whatever one likes, (within reason, of course). You are then going to have confidence in yourself, and this confidence gives you the assurance that you are capable of accomplishing perfectly well whatever you wish to do, --on condition that it is reasonable,--and whatever it is your duty to do.

So when you wish to do something reasonable, or when you have a duty to perform, always think that it is easy, and make the words difficult, impossible, I cannot, it is stronger than I, I cannot prevent myself from. . . , disappear from your vocabulary; they are not English. What is English is: "It is easy and I can ". By considering the thing easy it becomes so for you, although it might seem difficult to others. You will do it quickly and well, and without fatigue, because you do it without effort, whereas if you had considered it as difficult or impossible it would have become so for you, simply because you would have thought it so.

To these general suggestions which will perhaps seem long and even childish to some of you, but which are necessary, must be added those which apply to the particular case of the patient you are dealing with.

All these suggestions must be made in a monotonous and soothing voice (always emphasizing the essential words), which although it does not actually send the subject to sleep, at least makes him feel drowsy, and think of nothing in particular.

When you have come to the end of the series of suggestions you address the subject in these terms: "In short, I mean that from every point of view, physical as well as mental, you are going to enjoy excellent health, better health than that you have been able to enjoy up to the present. Now I am going to count three, and when I say 'Three', you will open your eyes and come out of the passive state in which you are now. You will come out of it quite naturally, without feeling in the least drowsy or tired, on the contrary, you will feel strong, vigorous, alert, active, full of life; further still, you will feel very cheerful and fit in every way. 'ONE--TWO--THREE--' At the word 'three' the subject opens his eyes, always with a smile and an expression of well-being and contentment on his face."

Sometimes,--though rarely,--the patient is cured on the spot; at other times, and this is more generally the case, he finds himself relieved, his pain or his depression has partially or totally disappeared, though only for a certain lapse of time.

In every case it is necessary to renew the suggestions more or less frequently according to your subject, being careful always to space them out at longer and longer intervals, according to the progress obtained until they are no longer necessary,--that is to say when the cure is complete.

Before sending away your patient, you must tell him that he carries within him the instrument by which he can cure himself, and that you are, as it were, only a professor teaching him to use this instrument, and that he must help you in your task. Thus, every morning before rising, and every night on getting into bed, he must shut his eyes and in thought transport himself into your presence, and then repeat twenty times consecutively in a monotonous voice, counting by means of a string with twenty knots in it, this little phrase:

"EVERY DAY, IN EVERY RESPECT, I AM GETTING BETTER AND BETTER." In his mind he should emphasize the words "in every respect" which applies to every need, mental or physical. This general suggestion is more efficacious than special ones.

Thus it is easy to realize the part played by the giver of the suggestions. He is not a master who gives orders, but a friend, a guide, who leads the patient step by step on the road to health. As all the suggestions are given in the interest of the patient, the unconscious of the latter asks nothing better than to assimilate them and transform them into autosuggestions. When this has been done, the cure is obtained more or less rapidly according to circumstances.

THE SUPERIORITY OF THIS METHOD

This method gives absolutely marvelous results, and it is easy to understand why. Indeed, by following out my advice, it is impossible to fail, except with the two classes of persons mentioned above, who fortunately represent barely 3 per cent of the whole. If, however, you try to put your subjects to sleep right away, without the explanations and preliminary experiments necessary to bring them to accept the suggestions and to transform them into autosuggestions you cannot and will not succeed except with peculiarly sensitive subjects, and these are rare. Everybody may become so by training, but very few are so sufficiently without the preliminary instruction that I recommend, which can be done in a few minutes.

Formerly, imagining that suggestions could only be given during sleep, I always tried to put my patient to sleep; but on discovering that it was not indispensable, I left off doing it in order to spare him the dread and uneasiness he almost always experiences when he is told that he is going to be sent to sleep, and which often makes him offer, in spite of himself, an involuntary resistance. If, on the contrary, you tell him that you are not going to put him to sleep as there is no need to do so, you gain his confidence. He listens to you without fear or any ulterior thought, and it often happens--if not the first time, anyhow very soon--that, soothed by the monotonous sound of your voice, he falls into a deep sleep from which he awakes astonished at having slept at all.

If there are sceptics among you--as I am quite sure there are--all I have to say to them is: "Come to my house and see what is being done, and you will be convinced by fact."

You must not however run away with the idea that autosuggestion can only be brought about in the way I have described. It is possible to make suggestions to people without their knowledge and without any preparation. For instance, if a doctor who by his title alone has a suggestive influence on his patient, tells him that he can do nothing for him, and that his illness is incurable, he provokes in the mind of the latter an autosuggestion which may have the most disastrous consequences; if however he tells him that his illness is a serious one, it is true, but that with care, time, and patience, he can be cured, he sometimes and even often obtains results which will surprise him.

Here is another example: if a doctor after examining his patient, writes a prescription and gives it to him without any comment, the remedies prescribed will not have much chance of succeeding; if, on the other hand, he explains to his patient that such and such medicines must be taken in such and such conditions and that they will produce certain results, those results are practically certain to be brought about.

If in this hall there are medical men or brother chemists, I hope they will not think me their enemy. I am on the contrary their best friend. On the one hand I should like to see the theoretical and practical study of suggestion on the syllabus of the medical schools for the great benefit of the sick and of the doctors themselves; and on the other hand, in my opinion, every time that a patient goes to see his doctor, the latter should order him one or even several medicines, even if they are not necessary. As a matter of fact, when a patient visits his doctor, it is in order to be told what medicine will cure him.

He does not realize that it is the hygiene and regimen which do this, and he attaches little importance to them. It is a medicine that he wants.

In my opinion, if the doctor only prescribes a regimen without any medicine, his patient will be dissatisfied; he will say that he took the trouble to consult him for nothing, and often goes to another doctor. It seems to me then that the doctor should always prescribe medicines to his patient, and, as much as possible, medicines made up by himself rather than the standard remedies so much advertised and which owe their only value to the advertisement. The doctor's own prescriptions will inspire infinitely more confidence than So and So's pills which anyone can procure easily at the nearest drug store without any need of a prescription.

HOW SUGGESTION WORKS

In order to understand properly the part played by suggestion or rather by autosuggestion, it is enough to know that the unconscious self is the grand director of all our functions. Make this believed, as I said above, that a certain organ which does not function well must perform its function, and instantly the order is transmitted. The organ obeys with docility, and either at once or little by little performs its functions in a normal manner. This explains simply and clearly how by means of suggestion one can stop haemorrhages, cure constipation, cause fibrous tumours to disappear, cure paralysis, tubercular lesions, varicose, ulcers, etc.

Let us take for example, a case of dental haemorrhage which I had the opportunity of observing in the consulting room of M. Gauth? a dentist at Troyes. A young lady whom I had helped to cure herself of asthma from which she had suffered for eight years, told me one day that she wanted to have a tooth out. As I knew her to be very sensitive, I offered to make her feel nothing of the operation. She naturally accepted with pleasure and we made an appointment with the dentist. On the day we had arranged we presented ourselves at the dentist's and, standing opposite my patient, I looked fixedly at her, saying: "You feel nothing, you feel nothing, etc., etc." and then while still continuing the suggestion I made a sign to the dentist. In an instant the tooth was out without Mlle. D---- turning a hair. As fairly often happens, a haemorrhage followed, but I told the dentist that I would try suggestion without his using a haemostatic, without knowing beforehand what would happen. I then asked Mlle. D---- to look at me fixedly, and I suggested to her that in two minutes the haemorrhage would cease of its own accord, and we waited. The patient spat blood again once or twice, and then ceased. I told her to open her mouth, and we both looked and found that a clot of blood had formed in the dental cavity.

How is this phenomenon to be explained? In the simplest way. Under the influence of the idea: "The haemorrhage is to stop", the unconscious had sent to the small arteries and veins the order to stop the flow of blood, and, obediently, they contracted naturally, as they would have done artificially at the contact of a haemostatic like adrenalin, for example.

The same reasoning explains how a fibrous tumour can be made to disappear. The unconscious having accepted the idea "It is to go" the brain orders the arteries which nourish it, to contract. They do so, refusing their services, and ceasing to nourish the tumour which, deprived of nourishment, dies, dries up, is reabsorbed and disappears.

THE USE OF SUGGESTION FOR THE CURE OF MORAL AILMENTS AND TAINTS EITHER CONGENITAL OR ACQUIRED

Neurasthenia, so common nowadays, generally yields to suggestion constantly practised in the way I have indicated. I have had the happiness of contributing to the cure of a large number of neurasthenics with whom every other treatment had failed. One of them had even spent a month in a special establishment at Luxemburg without obtaining any improvement. In six weeks he was completely cured, and he is now the happiest man one would wish to find, after having thought himself the most miserable. Neither is he ever likely to fall ill again in the same way, for I showed him how to make use of conscious autosuggestion and he does it marvelously well.

But if suggestion is useful in treating moral complaints and physical ailments, may it not render still greater services to society, in turning into honest folks the wretched children who people our reformatories and who only leave them to enter the army of crime. Let no one tell me it is impossible. The remedy exists and I can prove it.

I will quote the two following cases which are very characteristic, but here I must insert a few remarks in parenthesis. To make you understand the way in which suggestion acts in the treatment of moral taints I will use the following comparison. Suppose our brain is a plank in which are driven nails which represent the ideas, habits, and instincts, which determine our actions. If we find that there exists in a subject a bad idea, a bad habit, a bad instinct,--as it were, a bad nail, we take another which is the good idea, habit, or instinct, place it on top of the bad one and give a tap with a hammer--in other words we make a suggestion. The new nail will be driven in perhaps a fraction of an inch, while the old one will come out to the same extent. At each fresh blow with the hammer, that is to say at each fresh suggestion, the one will be driven in a fraction further and the other will be driven out the same amount, until, after a certain number of blows, the old nail will come out completely and be replaced by the new one. When this substitution has been made, the individual obeys it.

Let us return to our examples. Little M----, a child of eleven living at Troyes, was subject night and day to certain accidents inherent to early infancy. He was also a kleptomaniac, and, of course, untruthful into the bargain. At his mother's request I treated him by suggestion. After the first visit the accidents ceased by day, but continued at night. Little by little they became less frequent, and finally, a few months afterwards, the child was completely cured. In the same period his thieving propensities lessened, and in six months they had entirely ceased.

This child's brother, aged eighteen, had conceived a violent hatred against another of his brothers. Every time that he had taken a little too much wine, he felt impelled to draw a knife and stab his brother. He felt that one day or other he would end by doing so, and he knew at the same time that having done so he would be inconsolable. I treated him also by suggestion, and the result was marvelous. After the first treatment he was cured. His hatred for his brother had disappeared, and they have since become good friends and got on capitally together. I followed up the case for a long time, and the cure was permanent.

Since such results are to be obtained by suggestion, would it not be beneficial--I might even say indispensable--to take up this method and introduce it into our reformatories? I am absolutely convinced that if suggestion were daily applied to vicious children, more than 50 per cent could be reclaimed. Would it not be an immense service to render society, to bring back to it sane and well members of it who were formerly corroded by moral decay?

Perhaps I shall be told that suggestion is a dangerous thing, and that it can be used for evil purposes. This is no valid objection, first because the practice of suggestion would only be confided [by the patient] to reliable and honest people,--to the reformatory doctors, for instance,--and on the other hand, those who seek to use it for evil ask no one's permission.

But even admitting that it offers some danger (which is not so) I should like to ask whoever proffers the objection, to tell me what thing we use that is not dangerous? Is it steam? gunpowder? railways? ships? electricity? automobiles? aeroplanes? Are the poisons not dangerous which we, doctors and chemists, use daily in minute doses, and which might easily destroy the patient if, in a moment's carelessness, we unfortunately made a mistake in weighing them out?

A FEW TYPICAL CURES

This little work would be incomplete if it did not include a few examples of the cures obtained. It would take too long, and would also perhaps be somewhat tiring if I were to relate all those in which I have taken part. I will therefore content myself by quoting a few of the most remarkable.

Mlle. M---- D----, of Troyes, had suffered for eight years from asthma which obliged her to sit up in bed nearly all night, fighting for breath. Preliminary experiments show that she is a very sensitive subject. She sleeps immediately, and the suggestion is given. From the first treatment there is an enormous improvement. The patient has a good night, only interrupted by one attack of asthma which only lasts a quarter of an hour. In a very short time the asthma disappears completely and there is no relapse later on.

M. M----, a working hosier living at Sainte-Savine near Troyes, paralyzed for two years as the result of injuries at the junction of the spinal column and the pelvis. The paralysis is only in the lower limbs, in which the circulation of the blood has practically ceased, making them swollen, congested, and discolored. Several treatments, including the antisyphilitic, have been tried without success. Preliminary experiments successful; suggestion applied by me, and autosuggestion by the patient for eight days. At the end of this time there is an almost imperceptible but still appreciable movement of the left leg. Renewed suggestion. In eight days the improvement is noticeable. Every week or fortnight there is an increased improvement with progressive lessening of the swelling, and so on. Eleven months afterwards, on the first of November, 1906, the patient goes downstairs alone and walks 800 yards, and in the month of July, 1907, goes back to the factory where he has continued to work since that time, with no trace of paralysis.

M. A---- G----, living at Troyes, has long suffered from enteritis, for which different treatments have been tried in vain. He is also in a very bad state mentally, being depressed, gloomy, unsociable, and obsessed by thoughts of suicide. Preliminary experiments easy, followed by suggestion which produces an appreciable result from the very day. For three months, daily suggestions to begin with, then at increasingly longer intervals. At the end of this time, the cure is complete, the enteritis has disappeared, and his morals have become excellent. As the cure dates back twelve years without the shadow of a relapse, it may be considered as permanent. M. G----, is a striking example of the effects that can be produced by suggestion, or rather by autosuggestion. At the same time as I made suggestions to him from the physical point of view, I also did so from the mental, and he accepted both suggestions equally well. Every day his confidence in himself increased, and as he was an excellent workman, in order to earn more, he looked out for a machine which would enable him to work at home for his employer. A little later a factory owner having seen with his own eyes what a good workman he was, entrusted him with the very machine he desired. Thanks to his skill he was able to turn out much more than an ordinary workman, and his employer, delighted with the result, gave him another and yet another machine, until M. G----, who, but for suggestion, would have remained an ordinary workman, is now in charge of six machines which bring him a very hand some profit.

Mme. D----, at Troyes, about 30 years of age. She is in the last stages of consumption, and grows thinner daily in spite of special nourishment. She suffers from coughing and spitting, and has difficulty in breathing; in fact, from all appearances she has only a few months to live. Preliminary experiments show great sensitiveness, and suggestion is followed by immediate improvement. From the next day the morbid symptoms begin to lessen. Every day the improvement becomes more marked, the patient rapidly puts on flesh, although she no longer takes special nourishment. In a few months the cure is apparently complete. This person wrote to me on the 1st of January, 1911, that is to say eight months after I had left Troyes, to thank me and to tell me that, although pregnant, she was perfectly well.

I have purposely chosen these cases dating some time back, in order to show that the cures are permanent, but I should like to add a few more recent ones.

M. X----, Post Office clerk at Luneville. Having lost one of his children in January, 1910, the trouble produces in him a cerebral disturbance which manifests itself by uncontrollable nervous trembling. His uncle brings him to me in the month of June. Preliminary experiments followed by suggestion. Four days afterwards the patient returns to tell me that the trembling has disappeared. I renew the suggestion and tell him to return in eight days. A week, then a fortnight, then three weeks, then a month, pass by without my hearing any more of him. Shortly afterwards his uncle comes and tells me that he has just had a letter from his nephew, who is perfectly well. He has taken on again his work as telegraphist which he had been obliged to give up, and the day before, he had sent off a telegram of 170 words without the least difficulty. He could easily, he added in his letter, have sent off an even longer one. Since then he has had no relapse.

M. Y----, of Nancy, has suffered from neurasthenia for several years. He has aversions, nervous fears, and disorders of the stomach and intestines. He sleeps badly, is gloomy and is haunted by ideas of suicide; he staggers when he walks like a drunken man, and can think of nothing but his trouble. All treatments have failed and he gets worse and worse; a stay in a special nursing home for such cases has no effect whatever. M. Y---- comes to see me at the beginning of October, 1910. Preliminary experiments comparatively easy. I explain to the patient the principles of autosuggestion, and the existence within us of the conscious and the unconscious self, and then make the required suggestion. For two or three days M. Y---- has a little difficulty with the explanations I have given him. In a short time light breaks in upon his mind, and he grasps the whole thing. I renew the suggestion, and he makes it himself too every day. The improvement, which is at first slow, becomes more and more rapid, and in a month and a half the cure is complete. The ex-invalid who had lately considered himself the most wretched of men, now thinks himself the happiest.

M. E----, of Troyes. An attack of gout; the right ankle is inflamed and painful, and he is unable to walk. The preliminary experiments show him to be a very sensitive subject. After the first treatment he is able to regain, without the help of his stick, the carriage which brought him, and the pain has ceased. The next day he does not return as I had told him to do. Afterwards his wife comes alone and tells me that that morning her husband had got up, put on his shoes, and gone off on his bicycle to visit his yards (he is a painter). It is needless to tell you my utter astonishment. I was not able to follow up this case, as the patient never deigned to come and see me again, but some time afterward I heard that he had had no relapse.

Mme. T----, of Nancy. Neurasthenia, dyspepsia, gastralgia, enteritis, and pains in different parts of the body. She has treated herself for several years with a negative result. I treat her by suggestion, and she makes autosuggestions for herself every day. From the first day there is a noticeable improvement which continues without interruption. At the present moment this person has long been cured mentally and physically, and follows no regimen. She thinks that she still has perhaps a slight touch of enteritis, but she is not sure.

Mme. X----, a sister of Mme. T----. Acute neurasthenia; she stays in bed a fortnight every month, as it is totally impossible for her to move or work; she suffers from lack of appetite, depression, and digestive disorders. She is cured by one visit, and the cure seems to be permanent as she has had no relapse.

Mme. H----, at Maxille. General eczema, which is particularly severe on the left leg. Both legs are inflamed, above all at the ankles; walking is difficult and painful. I treat her by suggestion. That same evening Mme. H---- is able to walk several hundred yards without fatigue. The day after the feet and ankles are no longer swollen and have not been swollen again since. The eczema disappears rapidly.

Mme. F----, at Laneuveville. Pains in the kidneys and the knees. The illness dates from ten years back and is becoming worse every day. Suggestion from me, and autosuggestion from herself. The improvement is immediate and increases progressively. The cure is obtained rapidly, and is a permanent one.

Mme. Z----, of Nancy, felt ill in January, 1910, with congestion of the lungs, from which she had not recovered two months later. She suffers from general weakness, loss of appetite, bad digestive trouble, rare and difficult bowel action, insomnia, copious night-sweats. After the first suggestion, the patient feels much better, and two days later she returns and tells me that she feels quite well. Every trace of illness has disappeared, and all the organs are functioning normally. Three or four times she had been on the point of sweating, but each time prevented it by the use of conscious autosuggestion. From this time Mme. Z---- has enjoyed perfectly good health.

M. X----, at Belfort, cannot talk for more than ten minutes or a quarter of an hour without becoming completely aphonous. Different doctors consulted find no lesion in the vocal organs, but one of them says that M. X---- suffers from senility of the larynx, and this conclusion confirms him in the belief that he is incurable. He comes to spend his holidays at Nancy, and a lady of my acquaintance advises him to come and see me. He refuses at first, but eventually consents in spite of his absolute disbelief in the effects of suggestion. I treat him in this way nevertheless, and ask him to return two days afterwards. He comes back on the appointed day, and tells me that the day before he was able to converse the whole afternoon without becoming aphonous. Two days later he returns again to say that his trouble had not reappeared, although he had not only conversed a great deal but even sung the day before. The cure still holds good and I am convinced that it will always do so.

Before closing, I should like to say a few words on the application of my method to the training and correction of children by their parents.

The latter should wait until the child is asleep, and then one of them should enter his room with precaution, stop a yard from his bed, and repeat 15 or 20 times in a murmur all the things they wish to obtain from the child, from the point of view of health, work, sleep, application, conduct, etc. He should then retire as he came, taking great care not to awake the child. This extremely simple process gives the best possible results, and it is easy to understand why. When the child is asleep his body and his conscious self are at rest and, as it were, annihilated; his unconscious self however is awake; it is then to the latter alone that one speaks, and as it is very credulous it accepts what one says to it without dispute, so that, little by little, the child arrives at making of himself what his parents desire him to be.

CONCLUSION

What conclusion is to be drawn from all this?

The conclusion is very simple and can be expressed in a few words: We possess within us a force of incalculable power, which, when we handle it unconsciously is often prejudicial to us. If on the contrary we direct it in a conscious and wise manner, it gives us the mastery of ourselves and allows us not only to escape and to aid others to escape, from physical and mental ills, but also to live in relative happiness, whatever the conditions in which we may find ourselves.

Lastly, and above all, it should be applied to the moral regeneration of those who have wandered from the right path.

THOUGHTS AND PRECEPTS OF EMILE COUEI
taken down literally by Mme. Emile Leon, his disciple.

Do not spend your time in thinking of illness you might have, for if you have no real ones you will create artificial ones.

***

When you make conscious autosuggestions, do it naturally, simply, with conviction, and above all without any effort. If unconscious and bad autosuggestions are so often realized, it is because they are made without effort.

***

Be sure that you will obtain what you want, and you will obtain it, so long as it is within reason.

***

To become master of oneself it is enough to think that one is becoming so. . . . Your hands tremble, your steps falter, tell yourself that all that is going to cease, and little by little it will disappear. It is not in me but in yourself that you must have confidence, for it is in yourself alone that dwells the force which can cure you. My part simply consists in teaching you to make use of that force.

***

Never discuss things you know nothing about, or you will only make yourself ridiculous.

Things which seem miraculous to you have a perfectly natural cause; if they seem extraordinary it is only because the cause escapes you. When you know that, you realize that nothing could be more natural.

***

When the will and the imagination are in conflict, it is always the imagination which wins. Such a case is only too frequent, and then not only do we not do what we want, but just the contrary of what we want. For example: the more we try to go to sleep, the more we try to remember the name of some one, the more we try to stop laughing, the more we try to avoid an obstacle, while thinking that we cannot do so, the more excited we become, the less we can remember the name, the more uncontrollable our laughter becomes, and the more surely we rush upon the obstacle.

It is then the imagination and not the will which is the most important faculty of man; and thus it is a serious mistake to advise people to train their wills, it is the training of their imaginations which they ought to set about.

***

Things are not for us what they are, but what they seem; this explains the contradictory evidence of persons speaking in all good faith.

***

By believing oneself to be the master of one's thoughts one becomes so.

***

Everyone of our thoughts, good or bad, becomes concrete, materializes, and becomes in short a reality.

We are what we make ourselves and not what circumstances make us.

***

Whoever starts off in life with the idea: "I shall succeed", always does succeed because he does what is necessary to bring about this result. If only one opportunity presents itself to him, and if this opportunity has, as it were, only one hair on its head, he seizes it by that one hair. Further, he often brings about unconsciously or not, propitious circumstances.

He who on the contrary always doubts himself, never succeeds in doing anything. He might find himself in the midst of an army of opportunities with heads of hair like Absalom, and yet he would not see them and could not seize a single one, even if he had only to stretch out his hand in order to do so. And if he brings about circumstances, they are generally unfavorable ones. Do not then blame fate, you have only yourself to blame.

***

People are always preaching the doctrine of effort, but this idea must be repudiated. Effort means will, and will means the possible entrance of the imagination in opposition, and the bringing about of the exactly contrary result to the desired one.

***

Always think that what you have to do is easy, if possible. In this state of mind you will not spend more of your strength than just what is necessary; if you consider it difficult, you will spend ten, twenty times more strength than you need; in other words you will waste it.

***

Autosuggestion is an instrument which you have to learn how to use just as you would for any other instrument. An excellent gun in inexperienced hands only gives wretched results, but the more skilled the same hands become, the more easily they place the bullets in the target.

***

Conscious autosuggestion, made with confidence, with faith, with perseverance, realizes itself mathematically, within reason.

***

When certain people do not obtain satisfactory results with autosuggestion, it is either because they lack confidence, or because they make efforts, which is the more frequent case. To make good suggestions it is absolutely necessary to do it without effort. The latter implies the use of the will, which must be entirely put aside. One must have recourse exclusively to the imagination.

***

Many people who have taken care of their health all their life in vain, imagine that they can be immediately cured by autosuggestion. It is a mistake, for it is not reasonable to think so. It is no use expecting from suggestion more than it can normally produce, that is to say, a progressive improvement which little by little transforms itself into a complete cure, when that is possible.

***

The means employed by the healers all go back to autosuggestion, that is to say that these methods, whatever they are, words, incantations, gestures, staging, all produce in the patient the autosuggestion of recovery.

Every illness has two aspects unless it is exclusively a mental one. Indeed, on every physical illness a mental one comes and attaches itself. If we give to the physical illness the coefficient 1, the mental illness may have the coefficient 1, 2, 10, 20, 50, 100, and more. In many cases this can disappear instantaneously, and if its coefficient is a very high one, 100 for instance, while that of the physical ailment is 1, only this latter is left, a 101st of the total illness; such a thing is called a miracle, and yet there is nothing miraculous about it.

***

Contrary to common opinion, physical diseases are generally far more easily cured than mental ones.

Buffon used to say: "Style is the man." We would put in that: "Man is what he thinks". The fear of failure is almost certain to cause failure, in the same way as the idea of success brings success, and enables one always to surmount the obstacles that may be met with.

***

Conviction is as necessary to the suggester as to his subject. It is this conviction, this faith, which enables him to obtain results where all other means have failed.

***

It is not the person who acts, it is the method.

***

. . . Contrary to general opinion, suggestion, or autosuggestion can bring about the cure of organic lesions.

Formerly it was believed that hypnotism could only be applied to the treatment of nervous illnesses; its domain is far greater than that. It is true that hypnotism acts through the intermediary of the nervous system; but the nervous system dominates the whole organism. The muscles are set in movement by the nerves; the nerves regulate the circulation by their direct action on the heart, and by their action on the blood vessels which they dilate or contract. The nerves act then on all the organs, and by their intermediation all the unhealthy organs may be affected.

Docteur Paul Joire, Pres   ident of the Societe universelle d'Etudes psychiques (Bull. No. 4 of the S. L. P.)

***

. . . Moral influence has a considerable value as a help in healing. It is a factor of the first order which it would be very wrong to neglect, since in medicine as in every branch of human activity it is the spiritual forces which lead the world.

Docteur Louis Renon, Lecturing professor at the Faculty of Medicine of Paris, and doctor at the Necker Hospital.

***

. . . Never lose sight of the great principle of autosuggestion: Optimism always and in spite of everything, even when events do not seem to justify it.

Ren?de Drabois, (Bull. 11 of the S. L. P. A.)

***

Suggestion sustained by faith is a formidable force.

Docteur A. L., Paris, (July, 1920.)

To have and to inspire unalterable confidence, one must walk with the assurance of perfect sincerity, and in order to possess this assurance and sincerity, one must wish for the good of others more than one's own.

"Culture de la Force Morale", by C. Baudouin.

OBSERVATIONS ON WHAT AUTOSUGGESTION CAN DO

Young B----, 13 years old, enters the hospital in January 1912. He has a very serious heart complaint characterized by a peculiarity in the respiration; he has such difficulty in breathing that he can only take very slow and short steps. The doctor who attends him, one of our best practitioners, predicts a rapid and fatal issue. The invalid leaves the hospital in February, no better. A friend of his family brings him to me and when I see him I regard him as a hopeless case, but nevertheless I make him pass through the preliminary experiments which are marvelously successful. After having made him a suggestion and advised him to do the same thing for himself, I tell him to come back in two days. When he does so I notice to my astonishment a remarkable improvement in his respiration and his walking. I renew the suggestion and two days afterwards, when he returns the improvement has continued, and so it is at every visit. So rapid is the progress that he makes that, three weeks after the first visit, my little patient is able to go on foot with his mother to the plateau of Villers. He can breathe with ease and almost normally, he can walk without getting out of breath, and can mount the stairs, which was impossible for him before. As the improvement is steadily maintained, little B---- asks me if he can go and stay with his grandmother at Carignan. As he seems well I advise him to do so, and he goes off, but sends me news of himself from time to time. His health is becoming better and better, he has a good appetite, digests and assimilates his food well, and the feeling of oppression has entirely disappeared. Not only can he walk like everybody else, but he even runs and chases butterflies.

He returns in October, and I can hardly recognize him, for the bent and puny little fellow who had left me in May has become a tall upright boy, whose face beams with health. He has grown 12 centimeters and gained 19 lbs. in weight. Since then he has lived a perfectly normal life; he runs up and down stairs, rides a bicycle, and plays football with his comrades.

Mlle. X----, of Geneva, aged 13. Sore on the temple considered by several doctors as being of tubercular origin; for a year and a half it has refused to yield to the different treatments ordered. She is taken to M. Baudouin, a follower of M. Coueiat Geneva, who treats her by suggestion and tells her to return in a week. When she comes back the sore has healed.

Mlle. Z----, also of Geneva. Has had the right leg drawn up for 17 years, owing to an abscess above the knee which had had to be operated upon. She asks M. Baudouin to treat her by suggestion, and hardly has he begun when the leg can be bent and unbent in a normal manner. (There was of course a psychological cause in this case.)

Mme. Urbain Marie, aged 55, at Maxille. Varicose nicer, dating from more than a year and a half. First visit in September, 1915, and a second one a week later. In a fortnight the cure is complete.

Emile Chenu, 10 years old, Grande-Rue, 19 (a refugee from Metz). Some unknown heart complaint with vegetations. Every night loses blood by the mouth. Comes first in July, 1915, and after a few visits the loss of blood diminishes, and continues to do so until by the end of November it has ceased completely. The vegetations also seem to be no longer there, and by August, 1916, there had been no relapse.

M. Hazot, aged 48, living at Brin. Invalided the 15th of January, 1915, with specific chronic bronchitis, which is getting worse every day. He comes in to me in October, 1915. The improvement is immediate, and has been maintained since. At the present moment, although he is not completely cured, he is very much better.

M. B----, has suffered for 24 years from frontal sinus, which had necessitated eleven operations!! In spite of all that had been done the sinus persisted, accompanied by intolerable pains. The physical state of the patient was pitiable in the extreme; he had violent and almost continuous pain, extreme weakness; lack of appetite, could neither walk, read nor sleep, etc. His nerves were in nearly as bad a state as his body, and in spite of the treatment of such men as Bernheim of Nancy, Dejerine of Paris, Dubois of Bern, X---- of Strasburg, his ill health not only continued but even grew worse every day. The patient comes to me in September, 1915, on the advice of one of my other patients. From that moment he made rapid progress and at the present time (1921) he is perfectly well. It is a real resurrection.

M. Nagengast, aged 18, rue Sellier, 39. Suffering from Pott's disease. Comes to me in the beginning of 1914, having been encased for six months in a plaster corset. Comes regularly twice a week to the "seances," and makes for himself the usual suggestion morning and evening. Improvement soon shows itself, and in a short time the patient is able to do without his plaster casing. I saw him again in April, 1916. He was completely cured, and was carrying on his duties as postman, after having been assistant to an ambulance at Nancy, where he had stayed until it was done away with.

M. D----, at Jarville. Paralysis of the left upper eyelid. Goes to the hospital where he receives injections, as a result of which the eyelid is raised. The left eye was, however, deflected outwards for more than 45 degrees, and an operation seemed to be necessary. It was at this moment that he came to me, and thanks to autosuggestion the eye went back little by little to its normal position.

Mme. L----, of Nancy. Continuous pain in the right side of the face, which had gone on for 10 years. She has consulted many doctors whose prescriptions seemed of no use, and an operation is judged to be necessary. The patient comes to me on the 25th of July, 1916, and there is an immediate improvement. In about ten days' time the pain has entirely vanished, and up to the 20th of December, there had been no recurrence.

T---- Maurice, aged 8 and a half, at Nancy: club feet. A first operation cures, or nearly so, the left foot, while the right one still remains crippled. Two subsequent operations do no good. The child is brought to me for the first time in February, 1915; he walks pretty well, thanks to two contrivances which hold his feet straight. The first visit is followed by an immediate improvement, and after the second, the child is able to walk in ordinary boots. The improvement becomes more and more marked, by the 17th of April the child is quite well. The right foot, however, is not now quite so strong as it was, owing to a sprain which he gave it in February, 1916.

Mlle X----, at Blainville. A sore on the left foot, probably of specific origin. A slight sprain has brought about a swelling of the foot accompanied by acute pains. Different treatments have only had a negative effect, and in a little while a suppurating sore appears which seems to indicate caries of the bone. Walking becomes more and more painful and difficult in spite of the treatment. On the advice of a former patient who had been cured, she comes to me, and there is noticeable relief after the first visits. Little by little the swelling goes down, the pain becomes less intense, the suppuration lessens, and finally the sore heals over. The process has taken a few months. At present the foot is practically normal, but although the pain and swelling have entirely disappeared, the back flexion of the foot is not yet perfect, which makes the patient limp slightly.

Mme. R----, of Chavigny. Metritis dating from 10 years back. Comes at the end of July, 1916. Improvement is immediate, the pain and loss of blood diminish rapidly, and by the following 29th of September both have disappeared. The monthly period, which lasted from eight to ten days, is now over in four.

Mme. H----, rue Guilbert-de-Pivourt, at Nancy, aged 49. Suffers from a varicose ulcer dating from September, 1914, which has treated according to her doctor's advice, but without success. The lower part of the leg is enormous (the ulcer, which is as large as a two franc piece and goes right down to the bone, is situated above the ankle). The inflammation is very intense, the suppuration copious, and the pains extremely violent. The patient comes for the first time in April, 1916, and the improvement which is visible after the first treatment, continues without interruption. By the 18th of February, 1917, the swelling has entirely subsided, and the pain and irritation have disappeared. The sore is still there, but it is no larger than a pea and it is only a few millimeters in depth; it still discharges very slightly. By 1920 the cure has long been complete.

Mlle. D----, at Mirecourt, 16 years of age. Has suffered from attacks of nerves for three years. The attacks, at first infrequent, have gradually come at closer intervals. When she comes to see me on the 1st of April, 1917, she has had three attacks in the preceding fortnight. Up to the 18th of April she did not have any at all. I may add that this young lady, from the time she began the treatment, was no longer troubled by the bad headaches from which she had suffered almost constantly.

Mme. M----, aged 43, rue d'Amance, 2, Malzille. Comes at the end of 1916 for violent pains in the head from which she has suffered all her life. After a few visits they vanish completely. Two months afterwards she realized that she was also cured of a prolapse of the uterus which she had not mentioned to me, and of which she was not thinking when she made her autosuggestion. (This result is due to the words: "in every respect" contained in the formula used morning and evening.)

Mme. D----, Choisy-le-Roi. Only one general suggestion from me in July, 1916, and autosuggestion on her part morning and evening. In October of the same year this lady tells me that she is cured of a prolapse of the uterus from which she had suffered for more than twenty years. Up to April, 1920, the cure is still holding good. (Same remark as in the preceding case.)

Mme. Jousselin, aged 60, rue des Dominicains, 6. Comes on the 20th of July, 1917, for a violent pain in the right leg, accompanied by considerable swelling of the whole limb. She can only drag herself along with groans, but after the "seance," to her great astonishment, she can walk normally without feeling the least pain. When she comes back four days afterwards, she has had no return of the pain and the swelling has subsided. This patient tells me that since she has attended the "seances" she has also been cured of white discharges, and of enteritis from which she had long suffered. (Same remark as above.) In November the cure is still holding good.

Mlle. G. L.----, aged 15, rue du Montet, 88. Has stammered from infancy. Comes on the 20th of July, 1917, and the stammering ceases instantly. A month after I saw her again and she had had no recurrence.

M. Ferry (Euge), aged 60, rue de la Ce, 56. For five years has suffered from rheumatic pains in the shoulders and in the left leg. Walks with difficulty leaning on a stick, and cannot lift the arms higher than the shoulders. Comes on the 17th of September, 1917. After the first "seance," the pains vanish completely and the patient can not only take long strides but even run. Still more, he can whirl both arms like a windmill. In November the cure is still holding good.

Mme. Lacour, aged 63, chemin des Sables. Pains in the face dating from more than twenty years back. All treatments have failed. An operation is advised, but the patient refuses to undergo it. She comes for the first time on July 25th, 1916, and four days later the pain ceases. The cure has held good to this day.

Mme. Martin, Grande-Rue (Ville-Vieille), 105. Inflammation of the uterus of 13 years standing, accompanied by pains and white and red discharges. The period, which is very painful, recurs every 22 or 23 days and lasts 10-12 days. Comes for the first time on the 15th of November, 1917, and returns regularly every week. There is visible improvement after the first visit, which continues rapidly until at the beginning of January, 1918, the inflammation has entirely disappeared; the period comes at more regular intervals and without the slightest pain. A pain in the knee which the patient had had for 13 years was also cured.

Mme. Castelli, aged 41, living at Einville (M.-et M.). Has suffered from intermittent rheumatic pains in the right knee for 13 years. Five years ago she had a more violent attack than usual, the leg swells as well as the knee, then the lower part of the limb atrophies, and the patient is reduced to walking very painfully with the aid of a stick or crutch. She comes for the first time on the 5th of November, 1917. She goes away without the help of either crutch or stick. Since then she no longer uses her crutch at all, but occasionally makes use of her stick. The pain in the knee comes back from time to time, but only very slightly.

Mme. Meder, aged 52, at Einville. For six months has suffered from pain in the right knee accompanied by swelling, which makes it impossible to bend the leg. Comes for the first time on Dec. 7th, 1917. Returns on Jan. 4th, 1918, saying that she has almost ceased to suffer and that she can walk normally. After that visit of the 4th, the pain ceases entirely, and the patient walks like other people.

EMILE COUEI

EDUCATION AS IT OUGHT TO BE

It may seem paradoxical but, nevertheless, the Education of a child ought to begin before its birth.

In sober truth, if a woman, a few weeks after conception, makes a mental picture of the sex of the child she is going to bring forth into the world, of the physical and moral qualities with which she desires to see it endowed and if she will continue during the time of gestation to impress on herself the same mental image, the child will have the sex and qualities desired.

Spartan women only brought forth robust children, who grew to be redoubtable warriors, because their strongest desire was to give such heroes to their country; whilst, at Athens, mothers had intellectual children whose mental qualities were a hundredfold greater than their physical attributes.

The child thus engendered will be apt to accept readily good suggestions which may be made to him and to transform them into autosuggestion which later, will influence the course of his life. For you must know that all our words, all our acts, are only the result of autosuggestions caused, for the most part, by the suggestion of example or speech.

How then should parents, and those entrusted with the education of children avoid provoking bad autosuggestions and, on the other hand, influence good autosuggestions?

In dealing with children, always be even-tempered and speak in a gentle but firm tone. In this way they will become obedient without ever having the slightest desire to resist authority.

Above all--above all, avoid harshness and brutality, for there the risk is incurred of influencing an autosuggestion of cruelty accompanied by hate.

Moreover, avoid carefully, in their presence, saying evil of anyone, as too often happens, when, without any deliberate intention, the absent nurse is picked to pieces in the drawing-room.

Inevitably this fatal example will be followed, and may produce later a real catastrophe.

Awaken in them a desire to know the reason of things and a love of Nature, and endeavor to interest them by giving all possible explanations very clearly, in a cheerful, good-tempered tone. You must answer their questions pleasantly, instead of checking them with--"What a bother you are, do be quiet, you will learn that later."

Never on any account say to a child, "You are lazy and good for nothing" because that gives birth in him to the very faults of which you accuse him.

If a child is lazy and does his tasks badly, you should say to him one day, even if it is not true, "There this time your work is much better than it generally is. Well done". The child, flattered by the unaccustomed commendation, will certainly work better the next time, and, little by little, thanks to judicious encouragement, will succeed in becoming a real worker.

At all costs avoid speaking of illness before children, as it will certainly create in them bad autosuggestions. Teach them, on the contrary, that health is the normal state of man, and that sickness is an anomaly, a sort of backsliding which may be avoided by living in a temperate, regular way.

Do not create defects in them by teaching them to fear this or that, cold or heat, rain or wind, etc. Man is created to endure such variations without injury and should do so without grumbling.

Do not make the child nervous by filling his mind with stories of hob-goblins and were-wolves, for there is always the risk that timidity contracted in childhood will persist later.

It is necessary that those who do not bring up then children themselves should choose carefully those to whom they are entrusted. To love them is not sufficient, they must have the qualities you desire your children to possess.

Awaken in them the love of work and of study, making it easier by explaining things carefully and in a pleasant fashion, and by introducing in the explanation some anecdote which will make the child eager for the following lesson.

Above all impress on them that Work is essential for man, and that he who does not work in some fashion or another, is a worthless, useless creature, and that all work produces in the man who engages in it a healthy and profound satisfaction; whilst idleness, so longed for and desired by some, produces weariness, neurasthenia, disgust of life, and leads those who do not possess the means of satisfying the passions created by idleness, to debauchery and even to crime.

Teach children to be always polite and kind to all, and particularly to those whom the chance of birth has placed in a lower class than their own, and also to respect age, and never to mock at the physical or moral defects that age often produces.

Teach them to love all mankind, without distinction of caste. That one must always be ready to succor those who are in need of help, and that one must never be afraid of spending time and money for those who are in need; in short, that they must think more of others than of themselves.

In so doing an inner satisfaction is experienced that the egoist ever seeks and never finds.

Develop in them self-confidence, and teach that, before embarking upon any undertaking, it should be submitted to the control of reason, thus avoiding acting impulsively, and, after having reasoned the matter out, one should form a decision by which one abides, unless, indeed, some fresh fact proves you may have been mistaken.

Teach them above all that every one must set out in life with a very definite idea that he will succeed, and that, under the influence of this idea he will inevitably succeed. Not indeed, that he should quietly remain expecting events to happen, but because, impelled by this idea, he will do what is necessary to make it come true.

He will know how to take advantage of opportunities, or even perhaps of the single opportunity which may present itself, it may be only a single thread or hair, whilst he who distrusts himself is a Constant Guignard with whom nothing succeeds, because his efforts are all directed to that end.

Such a one may indeed swim in an ocean of opportunities, provided with heads of hair like Absalom himself, and he will be unable to seize a single hair, and often determines himself the causes which make him fail; whilst he, who has the idea of success in himself, often gives birth, in an unconscious fashion, to the very circumstances which produce that same success.

But above all, let parents and masters preach by example. A child is extremely suggestive, let something turn up that he wishes to do, and he does it.

As soon as children can speak, make them repeat morning and evening, twenty times consecutively:

"Day by day, in all respects, I grow better", which will produce in them an excellent physical, moral and healthy atmosphere.

If you make the following suggestion you will help the child enormously to eliminate his faults, and to awaken in him the corresponding desirable qualities.

Every night when the child is asleep, approach quietly, so as not to awaken him, to within about three or four feet from his bed. Stand there, murmuring in a low monotonous voice the thing or things you wish him to do.

Finally, it is desirable that all teachers should, every morning, make suggestions to their pupils, somewhat in the following fashion.

Telling them to shut their eyes, they should say: "Children, I expect you always to be polite and kind to everyone, obedient to your parents and teachers, when they give you an order, or tell you anything; you will always listen to the order given or the fact told without thinking it tiresome; you used to think it tiresome when you were reminded of anything, but now you understand very well that it is for your good that you are told things, and consequently, instead of being cross with those who speak to you, you will now be grateful to them.

"Moreover you will now love your work, whatever it may be; in your lessons you will always enjoy those things you may have to learn, especially whatever you may not till now have cared for.

"Moreover when the teacher is giving a lesson in class, you will now devote all your attention, solely and entirely to what he says, instead of attending to any silly things said or done by your companions, and without doing or saying anything silly yourself.

"Under these conditions as you are all intelligent, for, children, you are all intelligent, you will understand easily and remember easily what you have learned. It will remain embedded in your memory, ready to be at your service, and you will be able to make use of it as soon as you need it.

"In the same way when you are working at your lessons alone, or at home, when you are accomplishing a task or studying a lesson, you will fix your attention solely on the work you are doing, and you will always obtain good marks for your lessons."

This is the Counsel, which, if followed faithfully and truly from henceforth, will produce a race endowed with the highest physical and moral qualities.

Emile Couei

A SURVEY OF THE "SEANCES" AT M. COUEIS

The town thrills at this name, for from every rank of society people come to him and everyone is welcomed with the same benevolence, which already goes for a good deal. But what is extremely poignant is at the end of the seance to see the people who came in gloomy, bent, almost hostile (they were in pain), go away like everybody else; unconstrained, cheerful, sometimes radiant (they are no longer in pain!!). With a strong and smiling goodness of which he has the secret, M. Couei as it were, holds the hearts of those who consult him in his hand; he addresses himself in turn to the numerous persons who come to consult him, and speaks to them in these terms:

"Well, Madame, and what is your trouble? . . ."

Oh, you are looking for two many whys and wherefores; what does the cause of your pain matter to you? You are in pain, that is enough . . . I will teach you to get rid of that. . . .

And you, Monsieur, your varicose ulcer is already better. That is good, very good indeed, do you know, considering you have only been here twice; I congratulate you on the result you have obtained. If you go on doing your autosuggestions properly, you will very soon be cured. . . . You have had this ulcer for ten years, you say? What does that matter? You might have had it twenty and more, and it could be cured just the same.

And you say that you have not obtained any improvement? . . . Do you know why? . . . Simply because you lack confidence in yourself. When I tell you that you are better, you feel better at once, don't you? Why? Because you have faith in me. Just believe in yourself and you will obtain the same result.

Oh, Madame not so many details, I beg you! By looking out for the details you create them, and you would want a list a yard long to contain all your maladies. As a matter of fact, with you it is the mental outlook which is wrong. Well, make up your mind that it is going to get better and it will be so. It's as simple as the Gospel. . . .

You tell me you have attacks of nerves every week. . . . Well, from to-day you are going to do what I tell you and you will cease to have them. . . .

You have suffered from constipation for a long time? . . . What does it matter how long it is? . . . You say it is forty years? Yes, I heard what you said, but it is none the less true that you can be cured to-morrow; you hear, to-morrow, on condition, naturally, of your doing exactly what I tell you to do, in the way I tell you to do it. . . .

Ah! you have glaucoma, Madame. I cannot absolutely promise to cure you of that, for I am not sure that I can. That does not mean that you cannot be cured, for I have known it to happen in the case of a lady of Chalon-sur-Sa 魃 e and another of Lorraine.

Well, Mademoiselle, as you have not had your nervous attacks since you came here, whereas you used to have them every day, you are cured. Come back sometimes all the same, so that I may keep you going along the right lines.

The feeling of oppression will disappear with the lesions which will disappear when you assimilate properly; that will come all in good time, but you mustn't put the cart before the horse . . . it is the same with oppression as with heart trouble, it generally diminishes very quickly. . . .

Suggestion does not prevent you from going on with your usual treatment. . . . As for the blemish you have on your eye, and which is lessening almost daily, the opacity and the size are both growing less every day.

To a child (in a clear and commanding voice): "Shut your eyes, I am not going to talk to you about lesions or anything else, you would not understand; the pain in your chest is going away, and you won't want to cough any more."

Observation.--It is curious to notice that all those suffering from chronic bronchitis are immediately relieved and their morbid symptoms rapidly disappear. . . . Children, are very easy and very obedient subjects; their organism almost always obeys immediately to suggestion.

To a person who complains of fatigue: Well, so do I. There are also days when it tires me to receive people, but I receive them all the same and all day long. Do not say: "I cannot help it." "One can always overcome oneself."

Observation.--The idea of fatigue necessarily brings fatigue, and the idea that we have a duty to accomplish always gives us the necessary strength to fulfill it. The mind can and must remain master of the animal side of our nature.

The cause which prevents you from walking, whatever it is, is going to disappear little by little every day: you know the proverb: Heaven helps those who help themselves. Stand up two or three times a day supporting yourself on two persons, and say to yourself firmly: My kidneys are not so weak that I cannot do it, on the contrary I can. . . .

After having said: "Every day, in every respect, I am getting better and better," add: "The people who are pursuing me cannot pursue me any more, they are not pursuing me. . . ."

What I told you is quite true; it was enough to think that you had no more pain for the pain to disappear; do not think then that it may come back or it will come back. . . .

(A woman, sotto voice, "What patience he has! What a wonderfully painstaking man!")

ALL THAT WE THINK BECOMES TRUE FOR US. WE MUST NOT THEN ALLOW OURSELVES TO THINK WRONGLY.

THINK "MY TROUBLE IS GOING AWAY," JUST AS YOU THINK YOU CANNOT OPEN YOUR HANDS.

The more you say: "I will not," the more surely the contrary comes about. You must say: "It's going away," and think it. Close your hand and think properly: "Now I cannot open it." Try! (she cannot), you see that your will is not much good to you.

Observation.--This is the essential point of the method. In order to make auto-suggestions, you must eliminate the will completely and only address yourself to the imagination, so as to avoid a conflict between them in which the will would be vanquished.

To become stronger as one becomes older seems paradoxical, but it is true.

For diabetes: Continue to use therapeutic treatments; I am quite willing to make suggestions to you, but I cannot promise to cure you.

Observation.--I have seen diabetes completely cured several times, and what is still more extraordinary, the albumen diminish and even disappear from the urine of certain patients.

This obsession must be a real nightmare. The people you used to detest are becoming your friends, you like them and they like you.

Ah, but to will and to desire is not the same thing.

Then, after having asked them to close their eyes, M. Coueigives to his patients the little suggestive discourse which is to be found in "Self Mastery." When this is over, he again addresses himself to each one separately, saying to each a few words on his case:

To the first: "You, Monsieur, are in pain, but I tell you that, from to-day, the cause of this pain whether it is called arthritis or anything else, is going to disappear with the help of your unconscious, and the cause having disappeared, the pain will gradually become less and less, and in a short time it will be nothing but a moment."

To the second person: "Your stomach does not function properly, it is more or less dilated. Well, as I told you just now, your digestive functions are going to work better and better, and I add that the dilatation of the stomach is going to disappear little by little. Your organism is going to give back progressively to your stomach the force and elasticity it had lost, and by degrees as this phenomenon is produced, the stomach will return to its primitive form and will carry out more and more easily the necessary movements to pass into the intestine the nourishment it contains. At the same time the pouch formed by the relaxed stomach will diminish in size, the nutriment will not longer stagnate in this pouch, and in consequence the fermentation set up will end by totally disappearing."

To the third: "To you, Mademoiselle, I say that whatever lesions you may have in your liver, your organism is doing what is necessary to make the lesions disappear every day, and by degrees as they heal over, the symptoms from which you suffer will go on lessening and disappearing. Your liver then functions in a more and more normal way, the bile it secretes is alcaline and no longer acid, in the right quantity and quality, so that it passes naturally into the intestines and helps intestinal digestion."

To the fourth: "My child, you hear what I say; every time you feel you are going to have an attack, you will hear my voice telling you as quick as lightning: 'No, no! my friend, you are not going to have that attack, and it is going to disappear before it comes. . . .'"

To the fifth, etc., etc.

When everyone has been attended to, M. Coueitells those present to open their eyes, and adds: "You have heard the advice I have just given you. Well, to transform it into reality, what you must do is this: As long as you live, every morning before getting up, and every evening as soon as you are in bed, you must shut your eyes, so as to concentrate your attention, and repeat twenty times following, moving your lips (that is indispensable) and counting mechanically on a string with twenty knots in it the following phrase: 'Every day, in every respect, I am getting better and better.'"

There is no need to think of anything in particular, as the words "in every respect" apply to everything. This autosuggestion must be made with confidence, with faith, with the certainty of obtaining what is desired. The greater the conviction of the person, the greater and the more rapid will be the results obtained.

Further, every time that in the course of the day or night you feel any physical or mental discomfort, affirm to yourself that you will not consciously contribute to it, and that you are going to make it vanish; then isolate yourself as much as possible, and passing your hand over your forehead if it is something mental, or on whatever part that is painful if it is something physical, repeat very quickly, moving the lips, the words: "It is going, it is going . . ., etc., etc." as long as it is necessary. With a little practice, the mental or physical discomfort will disappear in about 20 to 25 seconds. Begin again every time it is necessary.

For this as for the other autosuggestions it is necessary to act with the same confidence, the same conviction, the same faith, and above all without effort.

M. Coueialso adds what follows: "If you formerly allowed yourself to make bad autosuggestions because you did it unconsciously, now that you know what I have just taught you, you must no longer let this happen. And if, in spite of all, you still do it, you must only accuse yourself, and say 'Mea culpa, mea maxima culpa.'"

And now, if a grateful admirer of the work and of the founder of the method may be allowed to say a few words, I will say. "Monsieur Coueishows us luminously that the power to get health and happiness is within us: we have indeed received this gift."

Therefore, suppressing, first of all, every cause of suffering created or encouraged by ourselves, then putting into practice the favorite maxim of Socrates: "Know thyself," and the advice of Pope: "That I may reject none of the benefits that Thy goodness bestows upon me," let us take possession of the entire benefit of autosuggestion, let us become this very day members of the "Lorraine Society of applied Psychology;" let us make members of it those who may be in our care (it is a good deed to do to them).

By this means we shall follow first of all the great movement of the future of which M. E. Coueiis the originator (he devotes to it his days, his nights, his worldly goods, and refuses to accept . . . but hush; no more of this! lest his modesty refuses to allow these lines to be published without alteration), but above all by this means we shall know exactly the days and hours of his lectures at Paris, Nancy and other towns, where he devotedly goes to sow the good seed, and where we can go too to see him, and hear him and consult him personally, and with his help awake or stir up in ourselves the personal power that everyone of us has received of becoming happy and well.

May I be allowed to add that when M. Coueihas charged an entrance fee for his lectures, they have brought in thousands of francs for the Disabled and others who have suffered through the war.

E. Vs----oer.

Note.--Entrance is free to the members of the Lorraine Society of applied Psychology.

EXTRACTS FROM LETTERS ADDRESSED TO M. COUEI
The final results of the English secondary Certificate have only been posted up these two hours, and I hasten to tell you about it, at least in so far as it concerns myself. I passed the viva voce with flying colors, and scarcely felt a trace of the nervousness which used to cause me such an intolerable sensation of nausea before the tests. During the latter I was astonished at my own calm, which gave those who listened to me the impression of perfect self-possession on my part. In short, it was just the tests I dreaded most which contributed most to my success. The jury placed me Second, and I am infinitely grateful to you for help, which undoubtedly gave me an advantage over the other candidates . . ., etc. (The case is that of a young lady, who, on account of excessive nervousness, had failed in 1915. The nervousness having vanished under the influence of autosuggestion, she passed successfully, being-placed 2nd out of more than 200 competitors.)

Mlle. V----, Schoolmistress, August, 1916.

***

It is with very great pleasure that I write to thank you most sincerely for the great benefit I have received from your method. Before I went to you I had the greatest difficulty in walking 100 yards, without being out of breath, whereas now I can go miles without fatigue. Several times a day and quite easily, I am able to walk in 40 minutes from the rue du Bord-de-l'Eau to the rue des Glacis, that is to say, nearly four kilometers. The asthma from which I suffered has almost entirely disappeared.

Yours most gratefully.

Paul Chenot, Rue de Strasbourg, 141 Nancy, Aug., 1917.

***

I do not know how to thank you. Thanks to you I can say that I am almost entirely cured, and I was only waiting to be so in order to express my gratitude. I was suffering from two varicose ulcers, one on each foot. That on the right foot, which was as big as my hand, is entirely cured. It seemed to disappear by magic. For weeks I had been confined to my bed, but almost immediately after I received your letter the ulcer healed over so that I could get up. That on the left foot is not yet absolutely healed, but will soon be so. Night and morning I do, and always shall, recite the prescribed formula, in which I have entire confidence. I may say also that my legs were as hard as a stone and I could not bear the slightest touch. Now I can press them without the least pain, and I can walk once more, which is the greatest joy.

Mme. Ligny, Mailleroncourt-Charette (Haute Sae), May, 1918.

***

N. B.--It is worthy of remark that this lady never saw M. Couei and that it is only thanks to a letter he wrote her on April 15th, that she obtained the result announced in her letter of May 3rd.

***

I am writing to express my gratitude, for thanks to you I have escaped the risk of an operation which is always a very dangerous one. I can say more: you have saved my life, for your method of autosuggestion has done alone what all the medicines and treatments ordered for the terrible intestinal obstruction from which I suffered for 19 days, had failed to do. From the moment when I followed your instructions and applied your excellent principles, my functions have accomplished themselves quite naturally.

Mme. S----, Pont Mousson, Feb., 1920.

***

I do not know how to thank you for my happiness in being cured. For more than 15 years I had suffered from attacks of asthma, which caused the most painful suffocations every night. Thanks to your splendid method, and above all, since I was present at one of your seances, the attacks have disappeared as if by magic. It is a real miracle, for the various doctors who attended me all declared that there was no cure for asthma.

Mme. V----, Saint-Di? Feb., 1920.

***

I am writing to thank you with all my heart for having brought to my knowledge, a new therapeutic method, a marvellous instrument which seems to act like the magic wand of a fairy, since, thanks to the simplest means, it brings about the most extraordinary results. From the first I was extremely interested in your experiments, and after my own personal success with your method, I began ardently to apply it, as I have become an enthusiastic supporter of it.

Docteur Vachet, Vincennes, May, 1920.

***

For 8 years I have suffered from prolapse of the uterus. I have used your method of autosuggestion for the last five months, and am now completely cured, for which I do not know how to thank you enough.

Mme. Soulier, Place du March Toul, May, 1920.

***

I have suffered terribly for 11 years without respite. Every night I had attacks of asthma, and suffered also from insomnia and general weakness which prevented any occupation. Mentally, I was depressed, restless, worried, and was inclined to make mountains out of mole hills. I had followed many treatments without success, having even undergone in Switzerland the removal of the turbinate bone of the nose without obtaining any relief. In Nov., 1918, I became worse in consequence of a great sorrow. While my husband was at Corfu (he was an officer on a warship), I lost our only son in six days from influenza. He was a delightful child of ten, who was the joy of our life; alone and overwhelmed with sorrow, I reproached myself bitterly for not having been able to protect and save our treasure. I wanted to lose my reason or to die. . . . When my husband returned (which was not until February), he took me to a new doctor who ordered me various remedies and the waters of Mont-Dore. I spent the month of August in that station, but on my return I had a recurrence of the asthma, and I realized with despair that "in every respect" I was getting worse and worse. It was then that I had the pleasure of meeting you. Without expecting much good from it, I must say, I went to your October lectures, and I am happy to tell you that by the end of November I was cured. Insomnia, feelings of oppression, gloomy thoughts, disappeared as though by magic, and I am now well and strong and full of courage. With physical health I have recovered my mental equilibrium, and but for the ineffaceable wound caused by my child's loss, I could say that I am perfectly happy. Why did I not meet you before? My child would have known a cheerful and courageous mother. Thank you again and again, M. Couei

Yours most gratefully,

E. Itier, Rue de Lille, Paris, April, 1920.

* * *

I can now take up again the struggle I have sustained for 30 years, and which had exhausted me.

I found in you last August a wonderful and providential help. Coming home to Lorraine for a few days, ill, and with my heart full of sorrow, I dreaded the shock which I should feel at the sight of the ruins and distress . . . and went away comforted and in good health. I was at the end of my tether, and unfortunately I am not religious. I longed to find some one who could help me, and meeting you by chance at my cousin's house you gave me the very help I sought. I can now work in a new spirit, I suggest to my unconscious to re-establish my physical equilibrium, and I do not doubt that I shall regain my former good health. A very noticeable improvement has already shown itself, and you will better understand my gratitude when I tell you that, suffering from diabetes with a renal complication, I have had several attacks of glaucoma, but my eyes are now recovering their suppleness. Since then my sight has become almost normal, and my general health has much improved.

Mlle. Th----, Professor at the Young Ladies' College at Ch----, Jan., 1920.

***

I read my thesis with success, and was awarded the highest mark and the congratulations of the jury. Of all these "honours" a large share belongs to you, and I do not forget it. I only regretted that you were not present to hear your name referred to with warm and sympathetic interest by the distinguished Jury. You can consider that the doors of the University have been flung wide open to your teaching. Do not thank me for it, for I owe you far more than you can owe me.

Ch. Baudouin, Professor at the Institut. J.-J. Rousseau, Geneva.

***

. . . I admire your courageousness, and am quite sure that it will help to turn many friends into a useful and intelligent direction. I confess that I have personally benefited by your teaching, and have made my patients do so too.

At the Nursing Home we try to apply your method collectively, and have already obtained visible results in this way.

Docteur Berillon, Paris, March, 1920.

***

. . . I have received your kind letter as well as your very interesting lecture.

I am glad to see that you make a rational connection between hetero and autosuggestion, and I note particularly the passage in which you say that the will must not intervene in autosuggestion. That is what a great number of professors of autosuggestion, unfortunately including a large number of medical men, do not realize at all. I also think that an absolute distinction should be established between autosuggestion and the training of the will.

Docteur Van Velsen, Brussels, March, 1920.

***

What must you think of me? That I have forgotten you? Oh, no, I assure you that I think of you with the most grateful affection, and I wish to repeat that your teachings are more and more efficacious; I never spend a day without using autosuggestion with increased success, and I bless you every day, for your method is the true one. Thanks to it, I am assimilating your excellent directions, and am able to control myself better every day, and I feel that I am stronger. . . . I am sure that you would find it difficult to recognize in this woman, so active in spite of her 66 years, the poor creature who was so often ailing, and who only began to be well, thanks to you and your guidance. May you be blessed for this, for the sweetest thing in the world is to do good to those around us. You do much, and do a little, for which I thank God.

Mme. M----, Cesson-Saint-Brieuc.

***

As I am feeling better and better since I began to follow your method of autosuggestion, I should like to offer you my sincere thanks. The lesion in the lungs has disappeared, my heart is better. I have no more albumen, in short I am quite well.

Mme. Lemaitre, Richemont, June, 1920.

***

Your booklet and lecture interested us very much. It would be desirable for the good of humanity that they should be published in several languages, so that they might penetrate to every race and country, and thus reach a greater number of unfortunate people who suffer from the wrong use of that all-powerful (and almost divine) faculty, the most important to man, as you affirm and prove so luminously and judiciously, which we call the Imagination.

I had already read many books on the will, and had quite an arsenal of formulae, thoughts, aphorisms, etc. Your phrases are conclusive. I do not think that ever before have "compressed tablets of self confidence."--as I call your healing phrases--been condensed into typical formulae in such an intelligent manner.

Don Enrique C----, Madrid.

***

Your pamphlet on "the self-control" contains very strong arguments and very striking examples. I think that the substitution of imagination for the power of the will is a great progress. It is milder and more persuasive.

A. F----, Reimiremont.

***

. . . I am happy to be able to tell you that my stomach is going on well. My metritis is also much better. My little boy had a gland in his thigh as big as an egg which is gradually disappearing.

E. L----, Saint-Clement (M-et-M.)

***

After I had undergone three operations in my left leg on account of a local tuberculosis, that leg became ill again in September, 1920. Several doctors declared that a new operation was necessary. They were about to open my leg from the knee to the ankle, and if the operation had failed, they would have had to perform an amputation.

As I had heard of your wondrous cures I came and saw you for the first time on the 6th of November, 1920. After the seance, I felt immediately a little better. I exactly followed your instructions and went three times to you. At the third time, I could tell you that I was completely cured.

Mme. L----, Henry (Lorraine).

***

. . . I will not wait any longer to thank you heartily for all the good I owe you. Autosuggestion has positively transformed me and I am now getting much better than I have been these many years. The symptoms of illness have disappeared little by little, the morbid symptoms have become rarer and rarer, and all the functions of the body work now normally. The result is that, after having become thinner and thinner during several years I have regained several kilos in a few months.

I cannot do otherwise than bless the Coueisystem.

L----, Cannes (A. M.).

***

Since 1917, my little girl has been suffering from epileptic crises. Several doctors had told me that about the age of 14 or 15 they would disappear or become worse. Having heard of you, I sent her to you from the end of December till May. Now her cure is complete, for during six months she has had no relapse.

Perrin (Charles), Essey-les Nancy.

***

For eight years, I had suffered from a sinking of the uterus. After having practiced your autosuggestion for five months, I have been radically cured. I don't know how to express my deep gratitude.

Mme. Soulie, 6, Place du March? Toul.

***

. . . Having suffered from a glaucoma since 1917, I have consulted two oculists who told me that only an operation would put an end to my sufferings, but unfortunately neither of them would assure me of a good result.

In the month of June, 1920, after having attended one of your seances I felt much better. In September I ceased to use the drops of pilocarpine which were the daily bread of my eye, and since then I have felt no more pain. My pupil is no more dilated, my eyes are normal; it is a real miracle.

Mme. M----, ?Soulosse.

***

A dedication to M. Coueiby the author of a medical treatise:

To M. Coueiwho knew how to dissect the human soul and to extract from it a psychologic method founded on conscious autosuggestion.

The master is entitled to the thanks of all; he has cleverly succeeded in disciplining the vagrant (Imagination) and in associating it usefully with the will.

Thus he has given man the means of increasing tenfold his moral force by giving him confidence in himself.

Docteur P. R., Francfort.

***

. . . It is difficult to speak of the profound influence exercised on me by your so kindly allowing me to view so often your work. Seeing it day by day, as I have done, it has impressed me more and more, and as you yourself said, there seems no limits to the possibilities and future scope of the principles you enunciate, not only in the physical life of children but also in possibilities for changing the ideas now prevalent in punishment of crime, in government, in fact, in all the relations of life. . . .

Miss Josephine M. Richardson.

***

. . . When I came, I expected a great deal, but what I have seen, thanks to your great kindness, exceeds greatly my expectation.

Montagu S. Monier-Williams, M. D., London.

FRAGMENTS FROM LETTERS Addressed to Mme. Emile Leon, Disciple of M. Couei

For some time I have been wanting to write and thank you most sincerely for having made known to me this method of autosuggestion. Thanks to your good advice the attacks of nerves to which I was subject, have entirely disappeared, and I am certain that I am quite cured. Further, I feel myself surrounded by a superior force which is an unfaltering guide, and by whose aid I surmount with ease the difficulties of life.

Mme. F----, Rue de Bougainville, 4, Paris.

***

Amazed at the results obtained by the autosuggestion which you made known to me, I thank you with all my heart.

For a year I have been entirely cured of articular rheumatism of the right shoulder from which I had suffered for eight years, and from chronic bronchitis which I had had still longer. The numerous doctors I had consulted declared me incurable, but thanks to you and to your treatment, I have found with perfect health the conviction that I possess the power to keep it.

Mme. L. T----, Rue du Laos, 4, Paris.

***

I want to tell you what excellent results M. Coueis wonderful method has produced in my case, and to express my deep gratitude for your valuable help. I have always been anaemic, and have had poor health, but after my husband's death I became much worse. I suffered with my kidneys, I could not stand upright, I also suffered from nervousness and aversions. All that has gone and I am a different person. I no longer suffer, I have more endurance, and I am more cheerful. My friends hardly recognize me, and I feel a new woman. I intend to spread the news of this wonderful method, so clear, so simple, so beneficent, and to continue to get from it the best results for myself as well.

M. L. D----, Paris, June, 1920.

***

I cannot find words to thank you for teaching me your good method. What happiness you have brought to me! I thank God who led me to make your acquaintance, for you have entirely transformed my life. Formerly I suffered terribly at each monthly period and was obliged to lie in bed. Now all is quite regular and painless. It is the same with my digestion, and I am no longer obliged to live on milk as I used, and I have no more pain, which is a joy. My husband is astonished to find that when I travel I have no more headaches, whereas before I was always taking tablets. Now, thanks to you, I need no remedies at all, but I do not forget to repeat 20 times morning and evening, the phrase you taught me: "Every day, in every respect, I am getting better and better."

B. P----, Paris, October, 1920.

***

In re-reading the method I find it more and more superior to all the developments inspired by it. It surpasses all that has been invented of so-called scientific systems, themselves based on the uncertain results of an uncertain science, which feels its way and deceives itself, and of which the means of observation are also fairly precarious in spite of what the learned say, M. Couei on the other hand, suffices for everything, goes straight to the aim, attains it with certainty and in freeing his patient carries generosity and knowledge to its highest point, since he leaves to the patient himself the merit of this freedom, and the use of a marvellous power. No, really, there is nothing to alter in this method. It is as you so strikingly say: a Gospel. To report faithfully his acts and words and spread his method, that is what must be done, and what I shall do myself as far as is in any way possible.

P. C.

***

I am amazed at the results that I have obtained and continue to obtain daily, by the use of the excellent method you have taught me of conscious autosuggestion. I was ill mentally and physically. Now I am well and am also nearly always cheerful. That is to say that my depression has given way to cheerfulness, and certainly I do not complain of the change, for it is very preferable, I assure you. How wretched I used to be! I could digest nothing; now I digest perfectly well and the intestines act naturally. I also used to sleep so badly, whereas now the nights are not long enough; I could not work, but now I am able to work hard. Of all my ailments nothing is left but an occasional touch of rheumatism, which I feel sure will disappear like the rest by continuing your good method. I cannot find words to express my deep gratitude to you.

Mme. Friry, Boulevard Malesherbes, Paris.

EXTRACTS FROM LETTERS Addressed to Mlle. Kaufmant, Disciple of M. Couei
As I have been feeling better and better since following the method of autosuggestion which you taught me, I feel I owe you the sincerest thanks, I am now qualified to speak of the great and undeniable advantages of this method, as to it alone I owe my recovery. I had a lesion in the lungs which caused me to spit blood. I suffered from lack of appetite, daily vomiting, loss of flesh, and obstinate constipation. The spitting of blood, lessened at once and soon entirely disappeared. The vomiting ceased, the constipation no longer exists, I have got back my appetite, and in two months I have gained nearly a stone in weight. In the face of such results observed, not only by parents and friends, but also by the doctor who has been attending me for several months, it is impossible to deny the good effect of autosuggestion and not to declare openly that it is to your method that I owe my return to life. I authorize you to publish my name if it is likely to be of service to others, and I beg you to believe me.

Yours most gratefully.

Jeanne Gilli, 15, Av. Borriglione, Nice, March, 1918.

***

I consider it a duty to tell you how grateful I am to you for acquainting me with the benefits of autosuggestion. Thanks to you, I no longer suffer from those agonizing and frequent heart stoppages, and I have regained my appetite which I had lost for months. Still more, as a hospital nurse, I must thank you from my heart for the almost miraculous recovery of one of my patients, seriously ill with tuberculosis, which caused him to vomit blood constantly and copiously. His family and myself were very anxious when heaven sent you to him. After your first visit the spitting of blood ceased, his appetite returned, and after a few more visits made by you to his sick bed, all the organs little by little resumed their normal functions. At last one day we had the pleasant surprise and joy of seeing him arrive at your private seance, where, before those present, he himself made the declaration of his cure, due to your kind intervention. Thank you with all my heart.

Yours gratefully and sympathetically,

A. Kettner, 26, Av. Borriglione, Nice, March, 1918.

***

. . . From day to day I have put off writing to you to thank you for the cure of my little Sylvain. I was in despair, the doctors telling me that there was nothing more to be done but to try the sanitorium of Arcachon or Juicoot, near Dunkirk. I was going to do so when Mine. Collard advised me to go and see you. I hesitated, as I felt sceptical about it; but I now have the proof of your skill, for Sylvain has completely recovered. His appetite is good, his pimples and his glands are completely cured, and what is still more extraordinary, since the first time that we went to see you he has not coughed any more, not even once; the result is, that since the month of June he has gained 6 lbs.; I can never thank you enough and I proclaim to everyone the benefits we have received.

Mme. Poirson, Liverdun, August, 1920.

***

How can I prove to you my deep gratitude? You have saved my life. I had a displaced heart, which caused terrible attacks of suffocation, which went on continually; in fact they were so violent that I had no rest day or night, in spite of daily injections of morphia. I could eat nothing without instant vomiting. I had violent pains in the head which became all swollen, and as a result I lost my sight. I was in a lamentable state and my whole organism suffered from it. I had abscesses on the liver. The doctor despaired of me after having tried everything; blood letting, cupping and scarifying, poultices, ice, and every possible remedy, without any improvement. I had recourse to your kindness on the doctor's advice.

After your first visits the attacks became less violent and less frequent, and soon disappeared completely. The bad and troubled nights became calmer, until I was able to sleep the whole night through without waking. The pains I had in the liver ceased completely. I could begin to take my food again, digesting it perfectly well, and I again experienced the feeling of hunger which I had not known for months. My headaches ceased, and my eyes, which had troubled me so much, are quite cured, since I am now able to occupy myself with a little manual work.

At each visit that you paid me, I felt that my organs were resuming their natural functions. I was not the only one to observe it, for the doctor who came to see me every week found me much better, and finally there came recovery, since I could get up after having been in bed eleven months. I got up without any discomfort, not even the least giddiness, and in a fortnight I could go out. It is indeed thanks to you that I am cured, for the doctor says that for all that the medicines did me, I might just as well have taken none.

After having been given up by two doctors who held out no hope of cure, here I am cured all the same, and it is indeed a complete cure, for now I can eat meat, and I eat a pound of bread every day. How can I thank you, for I repeat, it is thanks to the suggestion you taught me that I owe my life.

Jeanne Grosjean, Nancy, Nov., 1920.

***

. . . Personally the science of autosuggestion--for I consider it as entirely a science--has rendered me great services; but truth compels me to declare that if I continue to interest myself particularly in it, it is because I find in it the means of exercising true charity.

In 1915 when I was present for the first time at M. Coueis lectures, I confess that I was entirely sceptical. Before facts a hundred times repeated in my presence, I was obliged to surrender to evidence, and recognize that autosuggestion always acted, though naturally in different degrees, on organic diseases. The only cases (and those were very rare) in which I have seen it fail are nervous cases, neurasthenia or imaginary illness.

There is no need to tell you again that M. Couei like yourself, but even more strongly, insists on this point: "that he never performs a miracle or cures anybody, but that he shows people how to cure themselves." I confess that on this point I still remain a trifle incredulous, for if M. Coueidoes not actually cure people, he is a powerful aid to their recovery, in "giving heart" to the sick, in teaching them never to despair, in uplifting them, in leading them . . . higher than themselves into moral spheres that the majority of humanity, plunged in materialism, has never reached.

The more I study autosuggestion, the better I understand the divine law of confidence and love that Christ preached us: "Thou shalt love thy neighbor" and by giving a little of one's heart and of one's moral force to help him to rise if he has fallen and to cure himself if he is ill. Here also from my Christian point of view, is the application of autosuggestion which I consider as a beneficial and comforting science which helps us to understand that as the children of God, we all have within us forces whose existence we did not suspect, which properly directed, serve to elevate us morally and to heal us physically.

Those who do not know your science, or who only know it imperfectly, should not judge it without having seen the results it gives and the good it does. Believe me to be your faithful admirer.

M. L. D----, Nancy, November, 1920.

THE MIRACLE WITHIN

(Reprinted from the "Renaissance politique, littaire et artistique" of the 18th of December, 1920)

HOMAGE TO EMILE COUEI
In the course of the month of September, 1920, I opened for the first time the book of Charles Baudouin, of Geneva, professor at the Institute J. J. Rousseau in that town.

This work, published by the firm of Delachaux and Niestle, 26, rue Saint-Dominique, Paris, is called: "Suggestion et Autosuggestion". The author has dedicated it: "To Emile Couei the initiator and benefactor, with deep gratitude".

I read it and did not put down the book until I had reached the end.

The fact is that it contains the very simple exposition of a magnificently humanitarian work, founded on a theory which may appear childish just because it is within the scope of everyone. And if everyone puts it into practice, the greatest good will proceed from it.

After more than twenty years of indefatigable work, Emile Coueiwho at the present time lives at Nancy, where he lately followed the work and experiments of Li 鬧 ault, the father of the doctrine of suggestions, for more than twenty years, I say, Coueihas been occupied exclusively with this question, but particularly in order to bring his fellow creatures to cultivate autosuggestion.

At the beginning of the century Coueihad attained the object of his researches, and had disengaged the general and immense force of autosuggestion. After innumerable experiments on thousands of subjects, he showed the action of the unconscious in organic cases. This is new, and the great merit of this profoundly, modest learned man, is to have found a remedy for terrible ills, reputed incurable or terribly painful, without any hope of relief.

As I cannot enter here into long scientific details I will content myself by saying how the learned man of Nancy practises his method.

The chiselled epitome of a whole life of patient researches and of ceaseless observations, is a brief formula which is to be repeated morning and evening.

It must be said in a low voice, with the eyes closed, in a position favourable to the relaxing of the muscular system, it may be in bed, or it may be in an easy chair, and in a tone of voice as if one were reciting a litany.

Here are the magic words: "Every day, in every respect, I am getting better and better".

They must be said twenty times following, with the help of a string with twenty knots in it, which serves as a rosary. This material detail has its importance; it ensures mechanical recitation, which is essential.

While articulating these words, which are registered by the unconscious, one must not think of anything particular, neither of one's illness nor of one's troubles, one must be passive, just with the desire that all may be for the best. The formula "in every respect" has a general effect.

This desire must be expressed without passion, without will, with gentleness, but with absolute confidence.

For Emile Coueiat the moment of autosuggestion, does not call in the will in any way, on the contrary; there must be no question of the will at that moment, but the imagination, the great motive force infinitely more active than that which is usually invoked, the imagination alone must be brought into play.

"Have confidence in yourself," says this good counsellor, "believe firmly that all will be well". And indeed all is well for those who have faith, fortified by perseverance.

As deeds talk louder than words, I will tell you what happened to myself before I had ever seen M. Couei

I must go back then to the month of September when I opened M. Charles Baudouin's volume. At the end of a substantial exposition, the author enumerates the cure of illnesses such as enteritis, eczema, stammering, dumbness, a sinus dating from twenty years back which had necessitated eleven operations, metritis, salpingitis, fibrous tumours, varicose veins, etc., lastly and above all, deep tubercular sores, and the last stages of phthisis (case of Mme. D----, of Troyes, aged 30 years, who has become a mother since her cure; case was followed up, but there was no relapse). All this is often testified to by doctors in attendance on the patients.

These examples impressed me profoundly; there was the miracle. It was not a question of nerves, but of ills which medicine attacks without success. This cure of tuberculosis was a revelation to me.

Having suffered for two years from acute neuritis in the face, I was in horrible pain. Four doctors, two of them specialists, had pronounced the sentence which would be enough, of itself alone, to increase the trouble by its fatal influence on the mind: "Nothing to be done!" This "nothing to be done" had been for me the worst of autosuggestions.

In possession of the formula: "Every day, in every respect . . .", etc., I recited it with a faith which, although it had come suddenly, was none the less capable of removing mountains, and throwing down shawls and scarves, bareheaded, I went into the garden in the rain and wind repeating gently "I am going to be cured, I shall have no more neuritis, it is going away, it will not come back, etc. . . ." The next day I was cured and never any more since have I suffered from this abominable complaint, which did not allow me to take a step out of doors and made life unbearable. It was an immense joy. The incredulous will say: "It was all nervous." Obviously, and I give them this first point. But, delighted with the result, I tried the Couei Method for an oedema of the left ankle, resulting from an affection of the kidneys reputed incurable. In two days the oedema had disappeared. I then treated fatigue and mental depression, etc., and extraordinary improvement was produced, and I had but one idea: to go to Nancy to thank my benefactor.

I went there and found the excellent man, attractive by his goodness and simplicity, who has become my friend.

It was indispensable to see him in his field of action. He invited me to a popular "seance." I heard a concert of gratitude. Lesions in the lungs, displaced organs, asthma, Pott's disease (!), paralysis, the whole deadly horde of diseases were being put to flight. I saw a paralytic, who sat contorted and twisted in his chair, get up and walk. M. Coueihad spoken, he demanded confidence, great, immense confidence in oneself. He said: "Learn to cure yourselves, you can do so; I have never cured anyone. The power is within you yourselves, call upon your spirit, make it act for your physical and mental good, and it will come, it will cure you, you will be strong and happy". Having spoken, Coueiapproached the paralytic: "You heard what I said, do you believe that you will walk?" "Yes."--"Very well then, get up!" The woman got up, she walked, and went round the garden. The miracle was accomplished.

A young girl with Pott's disease, whose vertebral column became straight again after three visits, told me what an intense happiness it was to feel herself coming back to life after having thought herself a hopeless case.

Three women, cured of lesions in the lungs, expressed their delight at going back to work and to a normal life. Coueiin the midst of those people whom he loves, seemed to me a being apart, for this man ignores money, all his work is gratuitous, and his extraordinary disinterestedness forbids his taking a farthing for it. "I owe you something", I said to him, "I simply owe you everything. . . ." "No, only the pleasure I shall have from your continuing to keep well. . . ."

An irresistible sympathy attracts one to this simple-minded philanthropist; arm in arm we walked round the kitchen garden which he cultivates himself, getting up early to do so. Practically a vegetarian, he considers with satisfaction the results of his work. And then the serious conversation goes on: "In your mind you possess an unlimited power. It acts on matter if we know how to domesticate it. The imagination is like a horse without a bridle; if such a horse is pulling the carriage in which you are, he may do all sorts of foolish things and take you to your death. But harness him properly, drive him with a sure hand, and he will go wherever you like. Thus it is with the mind, the imagination. They must be directed for our own good. Autosuggestion, formulated with the lips, is an order which the unconscious receives, it carries it out unknown to ourselves and above all at night, so that the evening autosuggestion is the most important. It gives marvelous results."

When you feel a physical pain, add the formula "It is going away . . .", very quickly repeated, in a kind of droning voice, placing your hand on the part where you feel the pain, or on the forehead, if it is a mental distress.

For the method acts very efficaciously on the mind. After having called in the help of the soul for the body, one can ask it again for all the circumstances and difficulties of life.

There also I know from experience that events can be singularly modified by this process.

You know it to-day, and you will know it better still by reading M. Baudouin's book, and then his pamphlet: "Culture de la force morale", and then, lastly, the little succinct treatise written by M. Coueihimself: "Self Mastery." All these works may be found at M. Coueis.

If however I have been able to inspire in you the desire of making this excellent pilgrimage yourself, you will go to Nancy to fetch the booklet. Like myself you will love this unique man, unique by reason of his noble charity and of his love for his fellows, as Christ taught it.

Like myself also, you will be cured physically and mentally. Life will seem to you better and more beautiful. That surely is worth the trouble of trying for.

M. Burnat-Provins.

SOME NOTES ON THE JOURNEY OF M. COUEITO PARIS IN OCTOBER, 1919

The desire that the teachings of M. Coueiin Paris last October should not be lost to others, has urged me to write them down. Putting aside this time the numerous people, physically or mentally ill, who have seen their troubles lessen and disappear as the result of his beneficent treatment, let us begin by quoting just a few of his teachings.

Question.--Why is it that I do not obtain better results although I use your method and prayer?

Answer.--Because, probably, at the back of your mind there is an unconscious doubt, or because you make efforts. Now, remember that efforts are determined by the will; if you bring the will into play, you run a serious risk of bringing the imagination into play too, but in the contrary direction, which brings about just the reverse of what you desire.

Question.--What are we to do when something troubles us?

Answer.--When something happens that troubles you, repeat at once "No, that does not trouble me at all, not in the least, the fact is rather agreeable than otherwise." In short, the idea is to work ourselves up in a good sense instead of in a bad.

Question.--Are the preliminary experiments indispensable if they are unacceptable to the pride of the subject?

Answer.--No, they are not indispensable, but they are of great utility; for although they may seem childish to certain people, they are on the contrary extremely serious; they do indeed prove three things:

1. That every idea that we have in our minds becomes true for us, and has a tendency to transform itself into action.

2. That when there is a conflict between the imagination and the will, it is always the imagination which wins; and in this case we do exactly the contrary of what we wish to do.

3. That it is easy for us to put into our minds, without any effort, the idea that we wish to have, since we have been able without effort to think in succession: "I cannot," and then "I can."

The preliminary experiments should not be repeated at home; alone, one is often unable to put oneself in the right physical and mental conditions, there is a risk of failure, and in this case one's self-confidence is shaken.

Question.--When one is in pain, one cannot help thinking of one's trouble.

Answer.--Do not be afraid to think of it; on the contrary, do think of it, but to say to it, "I am not afraid of you."

If you go anywhere and a dog rushes at you barking, look it firmly in the eyes and it will not bite you; but if you fear it, if you turn back, he will soon have his teeth in your legs.

Question.--And if one does a retreat?

Answer.--Go backwards.

Question.--How can we realize what we desire?

Answer.--By often repeating what you desire: "I am gaining assurance," and you will do so; "My memory is improving," and it really does so; "I am becoming absolutely master of myself," and you find that you are becoming so.

If you say the contrary, it is the contrary which will come about.

What you say persistently and very quickly comes to pass (within the domain of the reasonable, of course).

Some testimonies:

A young lady to another lady: "How simple it is! There is nothing to add to it: he seems inspired. Do you not think that there are beings who radiate influence?"

. . . An eminent Parisian doctor to numerous doctors surrounding him: "I have entirely come over to the ideas of M. Couei"

. . . A Polytechnician, a severe critic, thus defines M. Couei "He is a Power."

. . . Yes, he is a Power of Goodness. Without mercy for the bad autosuggestions of the "defeatist" type, but indefatigably painstaking, active and smiling, to help everyone to develop their personality, and to teach them to cure themselves, which is the characteristic of his beneficent method.

How could one fail to desire from the depths of one's heart that all might understand and seize the "good news" that M. Coueibrings? "It is the awakening, possible for everyone, of the personal power which he has received of being happy and well."

It is, if one consents, the full development of this power which can transform one's life.

Then, and is it not quite rightly so? it is the strict duty (and at the same time the happiness) of those who have been initiated, to spread by every possible means the knowledge of this wonderful method, the happy results of which have been recognized and verified by thousands of persons, to make it known to those who suffer, who are sad, or who are overburdened . . . to all! and to help them to put it into practice.

Then, thinking of France, triumphant but bruised, of her defenders victorious but mutilated, of all the physical and moral suffering entailed by the war; may those who-have the power (the greatest power ever given to man is the power of doing good [Socrates]) see that the inexhaustible reservoir of physical and moral forces that the "Method" puts within our reach may soon become the-patrimony of all the nation and through it of humanity.

Mme. Emile Leon, Collaborator, in Paris, of M. Emile Couei

"EVERYTHING FOR EVERYONE"

By Mme. Emile Leon, Disciple of M. Couei

When one has been able to take advantage of a great benefit; when this benefit is within reach of everyone, although almost everyone is ignorant of it, is it not an urgent and absolute duty (for those who are initiated) to make it known to those around them? For all can make their own the amazing results of the "Emile CoueiMethod."

To drive away pain is much . . . but how much more is it to lead into the possession of a new life all those who suffer. . . .

Last April we had the visit of M. Emile Coueiat Paris, and here are some of his teachings:

Question.--Question of a theist: I think it is unworthy of the Eternal to make our obedience to his will, depend on what M. Coueicalls a trick or mechanical process: conscious autosuggestion.

M. Couei--Whether we wish it or not, our imagination always overrules our will, when they are in conflict. We can lead it into the right path indicated by our reason, by consciously employing the mechanical process that we employ unconsciously often to lead into the wrong.

And the thoughtful questioner says to herself: "Yes, it is true, in this elevated sphere of thought, conscious autosuggestion has the power to free us from obstacles created by ourselves, which might as it were put a veil between us and God, just as a piece of stuff, hanging in a window, can prevent the sun from coming into a room."

Question.--How ought one to set about bringing those dear to one who may be suffering, to make themselves good autosuggestions which would set them free?

Answer.--Do not insist or lecture them about it. Just remind them simply that I advise them to make an autosuggestion with the conviction that they will obtain the result they want.

Question.--How is one to explain to oneself and to explain to others that the repetition of the same words: "I am going to sleep. . . . It is going away . . ." etc., has the power to produce the effect, and above all so powerful an effect that it is a certain one?

Answer.--The repetition of the same words forces one to think them, and when we think them they become true for us and transform themselves into reality.

Question.--How is one to keep inwardly the mastery of oneself?

Answer.--To be master of oneself it is enough to think that one is so, and in order to think it, one should often repeat it without making any effort.

Question.--And outwardly, how is one to keep one's liberty?

Answer.--Self mastery applies just as much physically as mentally.

Question(Affirmation).--It is impossible to escape trouble or sadness, if we do not do as we should, it would not be just, and autosuggestion, cannot . . . and ought not to prevent just suffering.

M. Coueivery seriously and affirmatively).--Certainly and assuredly it ought not to be so, but it is so often . . . at any rate for a time.

Question.--Why did that patient who has been entirely cured, continually have those terrible attacks?

Answer.--He expected his attacks, he feared them . . . and so he provoked them; if this gentleman gets well into his mind the idea that he will have no more attacks, he will not have any; if he thinks that he will have them, he will indeed do so.

Question.--In what does your method differ from others.

Answer.--The differ not the will which rules us but the imagination; that is the basis, the fundamental basis.

Question.--Will you give me a summary of your "Method" for Mme. R----, who is doing an important work?

M. E. Couei--Here is the summary of the "Method" in a few words: Contrary to what is taught, it is not our will which makes us act, but our imagination (the unconscious). If we often do act as we will, it is because at the same time we think that we can. If it is not so, we do exactly the reverse of what we wish. Ex: The more a person with insomnia determines to sleep, the more excited she becomes; the more we try to remember a name which we think we have forgotten, the more it escapes us (it comes back only if, in your mind, you replace the idea: "I have forgotten", by the idea "it will come back"); the more we strive to prevent ourselves from laughing, the more our laughter bursts out; the more we determine to avoid an obstacle, when learning to bicycle, the more we rush upon it.

We must then apply ourselves to directing our imagination which now directs us; in this way we easily arrive at becoming masters of ourselves physically and morally.

How are we to arrive at this result? By the practice of conscious autosuggestion.

Conscious autosuggestion is based on this principle. Every idea that we have in our mind becomes true for us and tends to realize itself.

Thus, if we desire something, we can obtain it at the end of a more or less long time, if we often repeat that this thing is going to come, or to disappear, according to whether it is a good quality or a fault, either physical or mental.

Everything is included by employing night and morning the general formula: "Every day, in every respect, I am getting better and better".

Question.--For those who are sad--who are in distress?

Answer.--As long as you think: "I am sad", you cannot be cheerful, and in order to think something, it is enough to say without effort: "I do think this thing--"; as to the distress it will disappear, however violent it may be, that I can affirm.

A man arrives bent, dragging himself painfully along, leaning on two sticks; he has on his face an expression of dull depression. As the hall is filling up, M. E. Coueienters. After having questioned this man, he says to him something like this: "So you have had rheumatism for 32 years and you cannot walk. Don't be afraid, it's not going to last as long as that again."

Then after the preliminary experiments: "Shut your eyes, and repeat very quickly indeed, moving your lips, the words: 'It is going, it is going' (at the same time M. Coueipasses his hand over the legs of the patient, for 20 to 25 seconds). Now you are no longer in pain, get up and walk (the patient walks) quickly! quicker! more quickly still! and since you can walk so well, you are going to run; run! Monsieur, run!" The patient runs (joyously, almost as if he had recovered his youth), to his great astonishment, and also to that of the numerous persons present at the seance of April 27th, 1920. (Clinic of Dr. Berillon.)

A lady declares: "My husband suffered from attacks of asthma for many years, he had such difficulty in breathing that we feared a fatal issue; his medical adviser, Dr. X---- had given him up. He was almost radically cu red of his attacks, after only one visit from M. Couei.

A young woman comes to thank M. Coueiwith lively gratitude. Her doctor, Dr. Vachet, who was with her in the room, says that the cerebral anaemia from which she had suffered for a long while, which he had not succeeded in checking by the usual means, had disappeared as if by magic through the use of conscious autosuggestion.

Another person who had had a fractured leg and could not walk without pain and limping, could at once walk normally. No more pain, no more limping.

In the hall which thrills with interest, joyful testimonies break out from numerous persons who have been relieved or cured.

A doctor: "Autosuggestion is the weapon of healing". As to this philosopher who writes (he mentions his name), he relies on the genius of Couei

A gentleman, a former magistrate, whom a lady had asked to express his appreciation, exclaims in a moved tone: "I cannot put my appreciation into words--I think it is admirable--" A woman of the world, excited by the disappearance of her sufferings: "Oh, M. Couei one could kneel to you--You are the merciful God!" Another lady, very much impressed herself, rectifies: "No, his messenger".

An aged lady: It is delightful, when one is aged and fragile, to replace a feeling of general ill health by that of refreshment and general well-being, and M. E. Couei's method can, I affirm for I have proved it, produce this happy result, which is all the more complete and lasting since it relies on the all-powerful force which is within us.

A warmly sympathetic voice calls him the modest name he prefers to that of "Master": Professor Couei

A young woman who has been entirely won over: "M. Coueigoes straight to his aim, attains it with sureness, and, in setting free his patient, carries generosity and knowledge to its highest point, since he leaves to the patient himself the merit of his liberation and the use of a marvellous power".

A literary man, whom a lady asks to write a little "chef d'oeuvre" on the beneficent "Method" refuses absolutely, emphasizing the simple words which, used according to the Method, help to make all suffering disappear: "IT IS GOING AWAY--that is the chef-d'oeuvre!" he affirms.

And the thousands of sick folks who have been relieved or cured will not contradict him.

A lady who has suffered much declares: "In re-reading the 'Method' I find it more and more superior to the developments it has inspired; there is really nothing to take away nor add to this 'Method'--all that is left is to spread it. I shall do so in every possible way."

And now in conclusion I will say: Although M. Couei's modesty makes him reply to everyone:

I have no magnetic fluid--

I have no influence--

I have never cured anybody--

My disciples obtain the same results as myself--

"I can say in all sincerity that they tend to do so, instructed as they are in the valuable 'Method', and when, in some far distant future, the thrilling voice of its author called to a higher sphere can no longer teach it here below, the 'Method', his work, will help in aiding, comforting, and curing thousands and thousands of human beings: it must be immortal, and communicated to the entire world by generous France--for the man of letters was right, and knew how to illuminate in a word this true simple, and marvellous help in conquering pain: 'IT IS GOING AWAY--! There is the chef-d'oeuvre!'"

B. K. (Emile-Leon). Paris, June 6th, 1920.